The Rustacean's Path

From Zero to Systems Programming Hero in One Book

Booker Blunt

Rafael Sanders

Miguel Farmer

Boozman Richard

Chapter 1: Getting Started with Rust 11

Overview: Introduction to Rust and its Significance in the World of Systems Programming 11

What's Rust and Why Should You Learn It? 12

Installing Rust and Setting Up the Development Environment... 14

Hello, Rust! A Simple "Hello World" Program......... 17

Explanation of Rust's Memory Safety Features 18

Quick Tips: How to Set Up Rust on Your Machine and Your First Project Setup 19

Hands-on Project: Create a Simple Command-Line Application that Prints a Message to the Console .. 19

Chapter 2: Rust Fundamentals: Variables, Types, and Functions 21

Overview: Dive Deeper into Rust's Syntax and Fundamental Constructs.. 21

Variables and Constants in Rust 22

Understanding Data Types: Scalars and Compound Types 24

Functions and Rust's Ownership Model 26

Hands-on Project: Build a Simple Calculator that Takes User Input and Performs Basic Arithmetic Operations 28

Conclusion... 31

Chapter 3: Rust's Ownership and Borrowing: The Heart of Memory Safety.. 32

Overview: Introduction to Rust's Ownership Model, which Ensures Memory Safety without a Garbage Collector 32

The Ownership Rules: Moving, Borrowing, and References 33

The Concept of Lifetimes in Rust 37

How Rust Prevents Memory Leaks and Data Races 38

Hands-on Project: Create a Function that Manipulates a Vector of Strings and Showcases Borrowing and Ownership 39

Conclusion 41

Chapter 4: Rust Control Flow: Making Decisions and Loops 42

Overview: Covering Conditional Statements, Loops, and Pattern Matching 42

If, Else, and Match Statements 43

Loops: While, For, and Loop 46

Using Pattern Matching to Simplify Code 49

Hands-on Project: Create a Game of "Guess the Number" Using Conditional Statements and Loops 51

Conclusion 53

Chapter 5: Structs and Enums: Organizing Your Code 54

Overview: Learn How to Use Structs and Enums to Represent Complex Data Structures 54

What Are Structs and How to Use Them 55

Enums: Handling Discrete Values in a Type-Safe Way 58

Methods and Associated Functions 61

Hands-on Project: Build a Task Management System Using Structs and Enums....................................... **62**

Conclusion... **65**

Chapter 6: Error Handling in Rust: The Result and Option Types... 67

Overview: Master Error Handling with Rust's Result and Option Types... **67**

Why Rust Avoids Exceptions **68**

Using `Result` and `Option` for Safe Error Handling 69

Pattern Matching with `Result` and `Option` **71**

Hands-on Project: Implement a File Reader that Gracefully Handles Errors..................................... **73**

Conclusion... **75**

Chapter 7: Collections in Rust: Vectors, Hash Maps, and Strings 76

Overview: Working with Rust's Built-in Collections for Handling Lists and Maps of Data **76**

Vectors and HashMaps in Rust.............................. **77**

Handling Strings: `String` and `&str`..................... **82**

Iterators and For Loops with Collections **84**

Hands-on Project: Build a Contact Book Application that Stores and Retrieves Contacts Using a `HashMap` **85**

Conclusion... **88**

Chapter 8: Concurrency in Rust: Handling Multiple Threads 89

Overview: Rust's Approach to Safe Concurrency Using Threads **89**

How Rust's Ownership Model Helps Avoid Data Races... 90

Using Threads, Mutexes, and Channels................. 91

The Future of Concurrency: Async Programming in Rust 95

Hands-on Project: Implement a Multithreaded Program That Downloads Multiple Web Pages Simultaneously 96

Conclusion... 99

Chapter 9: Rust's Cargo: The Rust Package Manager 100

Overview: Learn How to Use Cargo to Manage Dependencies, Build, and Run Rust Projects........100

Creating Projects with Cargo 101

Managing Dependencies with Cargo.toml 103

Building and Testing with Cargo 105

Hands-on Project: Create a CLI Tool That Takes User Input and Runs Different Operations Based on Commands 108

Conclusion 111

Chapter 10: Rust for Web Development: Using Rocket for Building Web Apps...113

Overview: Introduction to Building Web Applications with Rust...113

Setting Up Rocket for Web Development.............114

Basic Routing, Handling Requests and Responses 116

Implementing Form Handling and Templates 119

Hands-on Project: Build a Simple CRUD Web Application with Rocket...121

Conclusion...124

Chapter 11: Rust for Networking: Building a Web Server 125

Overview: Learn the Fundamentals of Networking in Rust 125

Working with TCP and UDP Sockets in Rust..........125

Building a Simple HTTP Server 130

Asynchronous Networking with Tokio....................132

Hands-on Project: Create a Basic Chat Server That Handles Multiple Clients Using Rust's Async Features...135

Conclusion...138

Chapter 12: Rust for Embedded Systems Programming 139

Overview: Introduction to Rust in the World of Embedded Systems...139

Why Rust is Perfect for Low-Level Embedded Systems 140

Setting Up a Rust Environment for Embedded Systems 142

Accessing Hardware and Working with Memory Mapped I/O 144

Hands-on Project: Build a Basic LED Blinking Program for an Embedded System Using Rust 146

Conclusion...149

Chapter 13: Advanced Rust Features: Traits, Generics, and Macros..150

Overview: Go Deeper into Rust's Advanced Features that Provide Flexibility and Power 150

Understanding Traits and How They Enable Polymorphism..151

Working with Generics for Type Safety and Reusability..154

Using Macros to Reduce Repetitive Code 157

Hands-on Project: Create a Custom Collection Type with Generics, and Implement Several Methods Using Traits 160

Conclusion 162

Chapter 14: Testing and Benchmarking in Rust 163

Overview: Learn the Best Practices for Writing Tests and Benchmarks in Rust 163

Rust's Built-in Testing Framework 163

Benchmarking Code Performance with Criterion..168

Hands-on Project: Create a Simple Application and Write Tests to Ensure Correctness 169

Conclusion 172

Chapter 15: Rust in the Real World: From Small Projects to Production Systems 173

Overview: Transition from Learning Rust to Using It in Large-Scale Systems 173

Designing Systems with Rust: Performance and Safety 174

Integration with C and Other Languages 176

Deploying Rust Applications to the Cloud 178

Hands-on Project: Build a Real-World Microservice Using Rust, Deploy It, and Integrate It with a Front-End Application 182

Conclusion 184

Conclusion: Your Path to Mastery in Rust.................185

Review of Key Concepts Learned 185

Next Steps After Finishing the Book: Continuous Learning and Community Involvement.................189

Encouragement to Keep Building and Innovating ..191

Resources for Further Study: Books, Blogs, and Online Communities 192

Final Thoughts 194

How to Scan a Barcode to Get a Repository

1. **Install a QR/Barcode Scanner** – Ensure you have a barcode or QR code scanner app installed on your smartphone or use a built-in scanner in **GitHub, GitLab, or Bitbucket.**

2. **Open the Scanner** – Launch the scanner app and grant necessary camera permissions.

3. **Scan the Barcode** – Align the barcode within the scanning frame. The scanner will automatically detect and process it.

4. **Follow the Link** – The scanned result will display a **URL to the repository**. Tap the link to open it in your web browser or Git client.

5. **Clone the Repository** – Use **Git clone** with the provided URL to download the repository to your local machine.

Chapter 1: Getting Started with Rust

Overview: Introduction to Rust and its Significance in the World of Systems Programming

Rust is a modern, high-performance programming language that is gaining popularity across a wide range of industries. Initially created by Mozilla and designed by Graydon Hoare, Rust has carved a niche in systems programming due to its focus on memory safety, concurrency, and performance. While most programming languages rely on garbage collectors to manage memory, Rust's unique approach, based on its ownership system, allows developers to write safe and concurrent code without sacrificing performance.

Rust's value in systems programming comes from its ability to provide fine-grained control over system resources, like memory, without introducing risks like data races or undefined behavior. This makes it an ideal choice for developers who need to write efficient and reliable software, particularly for applications that involve low-level systems, web servers, embedded systems, and networking. But, what truly sets Rust apart is its approach to safety and performance. The Rust compiler enforces strict rules about memory usage during compile time, so developers can catch potential issues early, before they even run the program.

In this chapter, we'll explore why Rust is such a revolutionary language for systems programming, set up the development environment, and walk through writing your first Rust program. By the end of this chapter, you'll have a working understanding of what Rust is, why it's important, and how you can get started writing code in Rust.

What's Rust and Why Should You Learn It?

Rust is a compiled, statically typed language that is designed to be fast, safe, and concurrent. While it has many similarities to languages like C and C++, Rust brings modern features to the table that make it safer and more accessible. Here's a breakdown of Rust's key features that make it a strong contender for systems programming:

1. **Memory Safety**: One of Rust's most defining features is its ownership system. This system helps ensure that memory is managed safely without relying on garbage collection, which can cause performance bottlenecks. In Rust, every piece of memory is owned by exactly one variable at a time, and when that variable goes out of scope, the memory is automatically freed. This

eliminates common errors like dangling pointers and memory leaks.

2. **Concurrency without Fear**: Rust's concurrency model allows you to write safe multi-threaded code without the common pitfalls of race conditions. Rust's ownership system ensures that data is either mutable and owned by one thread or immutable and accessible by many, preventing data races during compile time. This gives you the power of parallelism without the headache.

3. **Zero-Cost Abstractions**: Rust provides high-level abstractions that do not come with the usual performance overhead. Features like pattern matching, iterators, and closures offer expressive, readable code without sacrificing performance.

4. **Interoperability**: Rust can easily integrate with other languages like C, which makes it a great choice for projects where you need to interface with existing codebases or low-level system APIs. Rust's Foreign Function Interface (FFI) enables seamless communication between Rust and C.

5. **Rich Ecosystem and Tools**: The Rust ecosystem is robust, with a package manager (Cargo), a testing framework, a documentation generator, and many libraries and tools available through the Rust community. The official documentation is second to none, making it easy to get up to speed quickly.

6. **Developer Experience**: Rust is known for its friendly and helpful compiler messages. The compiler's strict checks ensure that your code is memory safe, and the error messages you get are clear and provide guidance on how to fix issues. Rust's tooling, such as the integrated package manager (Cargo), makes dependency management and project setup easy.

Why should you learn Rust?

- **For Performance**: Rust is highly performant, often matching or exceeding C/C++ in speed. It's ideal for writing software where performance is critical, such as operating systems, game engines, and web servers.
- **For Safety**: The main reason to use Rust is its focus on safety. Rust eliminates entire classes of bugs that are common in C/C++, like buffer overflows and null pointer dereferencing.
- **For Concurrency**: Rust's safe concurrency model allows you to write multi-threaded applications that can take full advantage of modern multi-core processors without risking race conditions.
- **For Systems Programming**: Rust is a perfect fit for systems-level programming where you need low-level control over hardware and memory management, without sacrificing safety.

Rust has garnered a lot of attention from companies like Mozilla, Microsoft, Google, and Dropbox, who have adopted it for their performance-critical components. Learning Rust opens doors to working on cutting-edge projects in systems programming, embedded development, and web development.

Installing Rust and Setting Up the Development Environment

Before we dive into writing Rust programs, we need to set up the development environment. Fortunately, installing Rust is straightforward. Rust's official installation tool, `rustup`, manages Rust versions, tools, and related components for you, and it ensures you're using the latest stable version.

Step 1: Installing Rust

1. **Visit the Official Website**: Go to rust-lang.org and click on the "Get Started" button. This will guide you through the installation process.
2. **Install rustup**: `rustup` is an installer for the Rust programming language. It downloads and installs the latest stable version of Rust and sets up `cargo`, Rust's package manager and build system. On Windows, macOS, and Linux, simply run the following command in your terminal or command prompt:

```bash
curl --proto '=https' --tlsv1.2 -sSf https://sh.rustup.rs | sh
```

3. **Verify Installation**: Once the installation is complete, you can check that everything is working by running:

```bash
rustc --version
```

This will print the installed version of `rustc`, Rust's compiler.

Step 2: Setting Up Your Text Editor

While you can write Rust code in any text editor, using one that supports Rust's syntax and offers additional features like autocompletion, syntax highlighting, and inline error checking will make your experience much smoother. Here are some recommended editors:

- **VSCode**: A popular editor for Rust with excellent Rust extensions. Install the **Rust (rls)** extension for autocompletion and error checking.
- **IntelliJ IDEA with Rust Plugin**: IntelliJ IDEA is another great IDE that supports Rust through the Rust plugin.
- **Sublime Text**: If you prefer something lightweight, Sublime Text with the Rust Enhanced package is a good choice.
- **Vim/Neovim**: Vim users can install rust.vim and rust-analyzer for a smooth experience.

Step 3: Creating Your First Rust Project

With Rust installed and your editor set up, you can start coding! Rust comes with a powerful tool called `cargo`, which is Rust's build system and package manager. It handles tasks like building, running, and testing projects.

To create a new project, run the following commands in your terminal:

```bash

cargo new hello_rust
cd hello_rust
cargo run
```

This creates a new Rust project named `hello_rust` and runs it. You should see something like this:

```bash

Hello, world!
```

This is your first Rust program!

Hello, Rust! A Simple "Hello World" Program

Now that you've got everything set up, let's write a simple "Hello, World!" program in Rust.

1. **Create the Program**: In the `src/main.rs` file of the `hello_rust` directory, replace the existing content with the following:

    ```rust
    fn main() {
        println!("Hello, world!");
    }
    ```

2. **Run the Program**: Back in your terminal, run:

    ```bash
    cargo run
    ```

    You should see the output:

    ```
    Hello, world!
    ```

This program demonstrates Rust's basic syntax. `fn main()` is the entry point of every Rust program. `println!()` is a macro that outputs text to the console. Rust uses the `!` syntax to distinguish macros from functions.

Explanation of Rust's Memory Safety Features

One of the main reasons why Rust stands out is its ownership model, which prevents memory safety issues. In most languages like C or C++, you must manually manage memory, which can lead to issues like memory leaks and null pointer dereferencing. Rust automates memory management while ensuring safety.

Here's a breakdown of how Rust achieves memory safety:

1. **Ownership**: Every piece of memory in Rust is "owned" by a variable. When the variable goes out of scope, the memory is automatically freed. This prevents memory leaks.
2. **Borrowing**: Rust allows you to "borrow" a reference to data instead of passing ownership. Rust ensures that only one mutable reference or many immutable references can exist at any time, which prevents data races.
3. **Lifetimes**: Rust ensures that references do not outlive the data they point to by enforcing lifetimes, making sure references are always valid.

This system ensures that your code is memory-safe and that you avoid common bugs like dangling pointers and race conditions.

Quick Tips: How to Set Up Rust on Your Machine and Your First Project Setup

- **Check the Rust Version**: After installation, verify the Rust version by running `rustc --version` in your terminal.
- **Use `cargo`**: `cargo` is your best friend. It handles everything from project creation to running and testing. Use `cargo new <project_name>` to create new projects and `cargo run` to run them.
- **Leverage Rust's Documentation**: Rust has extensive documentation, including tutorials, API documentation, and more. If you're stuck, the Rust documentation is a great resource.
- **Take Advantage of Cargo.toml**: This file manages your project's dependencies. Use it to add libraries from the Rust package registry, **crates.io**.

Hands-on Project: Create a Simple Command-Line Application that Prints a Message to the Console

Let's create a simple project where we will ask the user for their name and then greet them.

1. **Create the Project**:

   In your terminal, type the following:

   ```bash
   cargo new greet_user
   cd greet_user
   ```

2. **Write the Code**:

Open the `src/main.rs` file and replace the existing code with:

```rust
use std::io;

fn main() {
    println!("Please enter your name:");

    let mut name = String::new();
    io::stdin().read_line(&mut name).expect("Failed to read line");

    println!("Hello, {}!", name.trim());
}
```

3. **Run the Project**:

Run the project with:

```bash
cargo run
```

The program will prompt you to enter your name, then it will greet you. Try it out!

Chapter 2: Rust Fundamentals: Variables, Types, and Functions

Overview: Dive Deeper into Rust's Syntax and Fundamental Constructs

In this chapter, we'll explore some of the fundamental building blocks of Rust programming. You've already seen the basic syntax in the first chapter, but now we'll break it down even further. The concepts of **variables**, **data types**, and **functions** are core to any Rust program, and understanding them thoroughly will make writing efficient and safe code much easier.

```
let x = 4);     tet nans     Ye addix19i
              attr= Wust     b- 120t 1
```

VARIABLES   **TVPES**   **FUNCTIONS**

We'll also delve into how Rust handles ownership and borrowing within functions, providing a deeper understanding of Rust's unique memory management system. By the end of this chapter, you'll have a firm grasp of how to declare and manipulate variables, use Rust's type system effectively, and work with functions in a safe and efficient manner.

This chapter will also feature a hands-on project: building a simple command-line calculator that takes user input and performs basic arithmetic operations. We'll go step by step, building the program while reinforcing the concepts you learn along the way.

Variables and Constants in Rust

Rust's approach to variables and constants is one of the first areas where we see how Rust prioritizes memory safety and efficiency. Let's break it down into two main concepts: **variables** and **constants**.

1. Variables in Rust: Variables in Rust are, by default, immutable. This means that once a value is assigned to a variable, it cannot be changed unless explicitly marked as mutable. This is a key feature that makes Rust's memory management so effective and reliable.

To declare a variable in Rust, you use the `let` keyword, followed by the variable name and its value. Here's an example:

```rust
let x = 5;
println!("The value of x is: {}", x);
```

In this example, `x` is an immutable variable, and the value 5 cannot be changed later in the program. If you try to change `x` after its declaration, the Rust compiler will throw an error, helping to prevent bugs.

To make a variable mutable, you simply add the `mut` keyword before the variable name:

```rust
rust
```

```rust
let mut x = 5;
println!("The value of x is: {}", x);
x = 10;
println!("The value of x is now: {}", x);
```

In this case, x is mutable, so it can be updated after its initial assignment.

2. Constants in Rust: Constants are variables that are bound to a value and cannot be changed during the program's execution. They are similar to immutable variables but have a few key differences:

- Constants must be explicitly typed (you cannot rely on Rust to infer the type).
- They are always constant, and their values are set at compile-time.
- Constants are declared with the const keyword.

Here's an example:

```rust
rust
```

```rust
const MAX_POINTS: u32 = 100_000;
println!("The maximum points are: {}", MAX_POINTS);
```

In this example, MAX_POINTS is a constant that holds the value 100_000. Notice that we use uppercase letters and underscores for formatting large numbers—this is a Rust convention to improve readability.

Understanding Data Types: Scalars and Compound Types

Rust's type system ensures memory safety, performance, and expressiveness. It can be broadly divided into **scalars** and **compound types**. Let's look at each of these in detail.

1. Scalar Types: Scalar types represent a single value. Rust provides several scalar types, each designed for specific kinds of data.

- **Integer Types**: These represent whole numbers. Rust offers several signed and unsigned integer types with different sizes (in bits). For example, `i32` (signed 32-bit) and `u64` (unsigned 64-bit).

rust

```rust
let a: i32 = 42;    // Signed integer
let b: u64 = 10000000000;    // Unsigned integer
```

- **Floating-Point Types**: Rust also has two floating-point types for representing numbers with decimals: `f32` and `f64`. The default is `f64`.

rust

```rust
let x: f64 = 3.14;
let y: f32 = 2.71;
```

- **Boolean Type**: The `bool` type represents a value of either `true` or `false`. It's commonly used in control flow statements (if, loops, etc.).

rust

```rust
let is_active: bool = true;
let is_odd: bool = false;
```

- **Character Type**: The `char` type represents a single character, and it is more powerful than typical character types in other languages. It can store Unicode characters, allowing for greater flexibility.

rust

```rust
let letter: char = 'A';
```

2. Compound Types: Compound types allow you to combine multiple values into one. Rust provides two types of compound types: **tuples** and **arrays**.

- **Tuples**: A tuple is a collection of values of different types. The values inside a tuple can be of any type and are accessed by their index.

rust

```rust
let person: (i32, &str, bool) = (25, "Alice", true);
println!("Age: {}, Name: {}, Active: {}", person.0,
person.1, person.2);
```

In this example, `person` is a tuple containing an integer, a string, and a boolean. You can access the tuple's elements using dot notation (`person.0` for the first element, `person.1` for the second, and so on).

- **Arrays**: An array in Rust is a collection of values of the same type. Arrays in Rust have a fixed length, meaning once you define an array, it cannot grow or shrink during the program's execution. To declare an array, use square brackets.

rust

```rust
let numbers: [i32; 5] = [1, 2, 3, 4, 5];
```

```rust
println!("First number: {}", numbers[0]);
```

In this example, `numbers` is an array of five integers. The type of the array is inferred as `[i32; 5]`, where `i32` is the type of the elements, and `5` is the length of the array.

Functions and Rust's Ownership Model

In Rust, functions are defined with the `fn` keyword. Functions are a critical part of any programming language, allowing you to break your program into smaller, reusable pieces of code. Rust functions can have parameters, return values, and even handle ownership of variables.

1. Defining Functions: Here's a simple function that takes two parameters, adds them, and returns the result:

rust

```rust
fn add(x: i32, y: i32) -> i32 {
    x + y
}
```

In this example:

- `fn` declares the function.
- `x: i32` and `y: i32` are the function parameters, both of type `i32`.
- `-> i32` specifies that the function returns a value of type `i32`.
- `x + y` is the function body, which returns the sum of `x` and `y`.

You can call this function like this:

```rust
let result = add(5, 3);
println!("The sum is: {}", result);
```

2. Rust's Ownership Model in Functions: Rust's ownership system plays a significant role in how variables are passed to and returned from functions. Understanding how ownership works will help you avoid memory bugs like dangling pointers and ensure your code is memory-efficient.

By default, when a variable is passed to a function, ownership is transferred to the function. This is called **moving** the variable. Here's an example:

```rust
fn takes_ownership(s: String) {
    println!("Ownership taken by the function: {}", s);
} // s is dropped here

fn main() {
    let my_string = String::from("Hello, Rust!");
    takes_ownership(my_string); // Ownership of my_string is moved to the function
    // println!("{}", my_string); // This will cause a compile-time error
}
```

After `my_string` is passed to the `takes_ownership` function, its ownership is moved, and you can no longer use `my_string` in the main function.

If you want to **borrow** a variable instead of moving it, you can use references. Rust enforces strict rules about borrowing to prevent data races:

```rust
rust

fn borrow_string(s: &String) {
    println!("Borrowed string: {}", s);
}

fn main() {
    let my_string = String::from("Hello, Rust!");
    borrow_string(&my_string); // Borrow a reference
to my_string
    println!("{}", my_string); // Still valid here
because no ownership was transferred
}
```

In this case, `borrow_string` takes a **reference** to `my_string`, meaning no ownership is transferred. The variable can still be used after the function call.

Hands-on Project: Build a Simple Calculator that Takes User Input and Performs Basic Arithmetic Operations

Let's create a simple calculator program that allows the user to perform basic arithmetic operations like addition, subtraction, multiplication, and division. This project will combine everything we've learned so far: variables, data types, functions, and input/output.

Step 1: Set Up the Project

Start by creating a new project using Cargo:

```bash
bash

cargo new calculator
cd calculator
```

Step 2: Write the Code

Open `src/main.rs` and replace the contents with the following code:

```rust
use std::io;

fn add(x: f64, y: f64) -> f64 {
    x + y
}

fn subtract(x: f64, y: f64) -> f64 {
    x - y
}

fn multiply(x: f64, y: f64) -> f64 {
    x * y
}

fn divide(x: f64, y: f64) -> f64 {
    if y == 0.0 {
        panic!("Cannot divide by zero!");
    }
    x / y
}

fn main() {
    println!("Enter first number:");

    let mut num1 = String::new();
    io::stdin().read_line(&mut num1).expect("Failed to read line");
    let num1: f64 = num1.trim().parse().expect("Please enter a valid number");

    println!("Enter second number:");

    let mut num2 = String::new();
    io::stdin().read_line(&mut num2).expect("Failed to read line");
```

```
    let num2: f64 =
num2.trim().parse().expect("Please enter a valid
number");

    println!("Choose an operation (+, -, *, /):");
    let mut operation = String::new();
    io::stdin().read_line(&mut
operation).expect("Failed to read line");
    let operation = operation.trim();

    let result = match operation {
        "+" => add(num1, num2),
        "-" => subtract(num1, num2),
        "*" => multiply(num1, num2),
        "/" => divide(num1, num2),
        _ => {
            println!("Invalid operation!");
            return;
        }
    };

    println!("The result is: {}", result);
}
```

Step 3: Explanation

In this code:

- We define four functions (add, subtract, multiply, divide) to perform basic arithmetic operations.
- We use std::io to read user input from the console.
- The program prompts the user to enter two numbers and then choose an operation.
- We use pattern matching (match) to determine which operation to perform based on the user's input.
- The program performs the operation and prints the result.

Step 4: Run the Program

Compile and run the program:

```bash
cargo run
```

Test the calculator by entering numbers and choosing operations. The program will display the result of the selected operation.

Conclusion

In this chapter, you've learned how to declare and use variables and constants, understand Rust's type system, and work with functions. You also tackled a hands-on project where you built a simple calculator that uses these fundamental concepts. With these foundations, you're well on your way to mastering Rust and moving on to more advanced topics in systems programming. Stay tuned for the next chapter, where we will dive deeper into Rust's ownership system and explore memory safety in greater detail!

Chapter 3: Rust's Ownership and Borrowing: The Heart of Memory Safety

Overview: Introduction to Rust's Ownership Model, which Ensures Memory Safety without a Garbage Collector

Rust's ownership system is the cornerstone of its memory safety features. It guarantees memory safety while avoiding the performance overhead of garbage collection, which is a common feature in many modern programming languages. Unlike languages that depend on a garbage collector to automatically manage memory, Rust requires developers to explicitly manage memory through its ownership, borrowing, and references system.

At first glance, this may seem like an added complexity, but Rust's ownership model is designed to prevent common issues like **dangling pointers, double frees**, and **data races**, all of which are frequent pitfalls in systems programming. With the ownership system in place, Rust is able to ensure that memory is automatically and safely cleaned up once it is no longer needed, all while giving developers full control over memory management.

In this chapter, we'll take a deep dive into how Rust's ownership works, including the rules governing **ownership**, **borrowing**, and **references**. We'll also explore the concept of **lifetimes** and how Rust uses them to track how long references to data remain valid. By the end of the chapter, you will have a thorough understanding of these core principles and be able to apply them to your own Rust projects.

The Ownership Rules: Moving, Borrowing, and References

Rust's ownership system is built around three primary rules, which ensure that memory is managed correctly and safely. These rules govern how variables are treated when they are passed between functions or used in different parts of your program.

1. Ownership in Rust

Every piece of data in Rust has a single owner, and when the owner goes out of scope, the memory used by that data is automatically freed. This system ensures that there are no memory leaks or invalid memory accesses. The owner of a piece of data is the variable that holds the value.

Here's a simple example to illustrate how ownership works in Rust:

```rust
fn main() {
    let s1 = String::from("Hello, Rust!");
    let s2 = s1;  // Ownership of the String is moved
to s2

    // println!("{}", s1);  // This would result in a
compile-time error because s1 no longer owns the
string
    println!("{}", s2);  // This is valid because s2
owns the string
}
```

In this example:

- The variable s1 is the **owner** of the String object.
- When we assign s1 to s2, the ownership of the String is **moved** to s2. After this move, s1 is no longer valid, and attempting to use it would result in a compile-time error.

The **move** of ownership happens automatically. Rust does this to prevent the situation where two variables try to access the same memory, which could lead to **double freeing** the memory or having one variable access invalid memory.

2. Borrowing in Rust

Borrowing allows one variable to access data without taking ownership of it. Rust allows two types of borrowing:

- **Immutable Borrowing**: Multiple parts of the program can borrow a piece of data immutably, meaning they can read the data but cannot modify it.
- **Mutable Borrowing**: Only one part of the program can borrow data mutably at a time, ensuring that the data can be safely modified.

Let's look at both types of borrowing in action.

Immutable Borrowing:

```rust
fn main() {
    let s1 = String::from("Hello, world!");
    let s2 = &s1;   // Immutable borrow
```

```
    println!("{}", s1);   // Valid: s1 can still be
used
    println!("{}", s2);   // Valid: s2 can read the
data
}
```

In this example:

- s2 **borrows** s1 immutably, meaning it can read s1 but cannot modify it.
- After borrowing, s1 remains valid, and both s1 and s2 can be used in the program.

Mutable Borrowing:

rust

```
fn main() {
    let mut s1 = String::from("Hello, world!");
    let s2 = &mut s1;   // Mutable borrow

    // println!("{}", s1);   // This would cause a
compile-time error because s1 is already mutably
borrowed
    s2.push_str(" - Rust!");   // s2 can modify the
data
    println!("{}", s2);   // Valid: s2 can access and
modify the data
}
```

In this example:

- s2 **mutably borrows** s1, meaning it can modify the value of s1.
- While s2 is borrowing s1 mutably, no other part of the program can access s1` either mutably or immutably.

- This prevents data races and ensures that no two parts of the program can simultaneously modify the same data.

3. References

References are pointers to data, and they are used to enable borrowing. There are two kinds of references:

- **Immutable references**: Multiple parts of your program can borrow data as immutable references at the same time.
- **Mutable references**: Only one part of your program can borrow data as a mutable reference at any given time.

rust

```rust
fn main() {
    let s1 = String::from("Hello, Rust!");
    let s2 = &s1;  // Immutable reference
    let s3 = &s1;  // Another immutable reference

    println!("s2: {}", s2);  // Valid: we can have
multiple immutable references
    println!("s3: {}", s3);  // Valid: we can have
multiple immutable references
}
```

Here:

- Both s2 and s3 are **immutable references** to s1, and Rust allows this because the data is not being modified.
- If we tried to create a mutable reference while immutable references existed, Rust would reject the code at compile time.

The Concept of Lifetimes in Rust

In Rust, **lifetimes** are a way of describing the scope for which a reference is valid. Rust uses lifetimes to ensure that references never outlive the data they point to, which prevents **dangling references** (references that point to invalid memory).

Rust's compiler uses lifetimes to enforce these rules. In most cases, the compiler can infer lifetimes automatically, but in some cases, you may need to annotate lifetimes explicitly.

Here's an example that illustrates how lifetimes work:

rust

```rust
fn longest<'a>(s1: &'a str, s2: &'a str) -> &'a str {
    if s1.len() > s2.len() {
        s1
    } else {
        s2
    }
}

fn main() {
    let s1 = String::from("long string");
    let s2 = String::from("short");

    let result = longest(&s1, &s2);
    println!("The longest string is: {}", result);
}
```

In this code:

- The function `longest` takes two string slices (`&str`), and the `'a` lifetime annotation ensures that the references `s1` and `s2` must live at least as long as the reference returned by the function.

- Rust ensures that the references passed to `longest` don't outlive the data they point to.

This prevents the program from attempting to return a reference to data that no longer exists (i.e., data that has gone out of scope).

How Rust Prevents Memory Leaks and Data Races

Rust's ownership and borrowing rules work together to prevent common memory errors that can lead to memory leaks or data races.

- **Memory Leaks**: A memory leak occurs when a program allocates memory but fails to deallocate it, leaving it unused but still consuming system resources. In Rust, memory is automatically freed when the owner of the data goes out of scope. Because of the ownership model, you don't need to manually deallocate memory, and Rust guarantees that memory is freed correctly when it is no longer needed.
- **Data Races**: A data race happens when multiple threads access the same data simultaneously, and at least one of them modifies the data. This can lead to unpredictable behavior, such as corruption of the data or crashes. Rust prevents data races by enforcing strict rules about **borrowing** and **ownership**. The Rust compiler ensures that data is either accessed by one thread mutably or by multiple threads immutably, but never both at the same time. This eliminates the possibility of data races in safe Rust code.

Hands-on Project: Create a Function that Manipulates a Vector of Strings and Showcases Borrowing and Ownership

Now that you understand the theory behind Rust's ownership and borrowing, let's apply it in a practical project. We'll create a function that manipulates a `Vec<String>` (a growable list of strings), demonstrating how ownership and borrowing work.

Step 1: Set Up the Project

Create a new project using Cargo:

```bash
cargo new string_manipulator
cd string_manipulator
```

Step 2: Write the Code

In the `src/main.rs` file, write the following code:

```rust
fn capitalize_first_word(s: &mut String) {
    if let Some(first_space) = s.find(' ') {
        let first_word = &s[0..first_space];
        let capitalized = first_word.to_uppercase();
        s.replace_range(0..first_space,
&capitalized);
    }
}

fn main() {
    let mut sentences = Vec::new();
    sentences.push(String::from("hello world"));
    sentences.push(String::from("rust is great"));

    println!("Before manipulation: {:?}", sentences);
```

```
    // Borrowing mutable references to manipulate the
vectors
    for sentence in &mut sentences {
        capitalize_first_word(sentence);
    }

    println!("After manipulation: {:?}", sentences);
}
```

Step 3: Explanation

Here's how this code demonstrates ownership and borrowing:

- We declare a mutable vector `sentences` that holds `String` objects.
- The function `capitalize_first_word` borrows a mutable reference (`&mut String`) to modify the string in place.
- Inside the function, we capitalize the first word of the sentence using Rust's string manipulation methods.
- In the `main` function, we loop through the vector of sentences and pass mutable references to `capitalize_first_word`.

Step 4: Run the Program

Now, run the program with:

```bash
cargo run
```

The program should print the following output:

```less
Before manipulation: ["hello world", "rust is great"]
After manipulation: ["HELLO world", "RUST is great"]
```

In this project:

- We've shown how **mutable borrowing** works by passing a mutable reference to each string in the vector.
- We've manipulated the data through the mutable references, and Rust ensures that there's no conflict with ownership or other references.

Conclusion

In this chapter, you learned about the heart of Rust's memory safety system—its ownership and borrowing model. You now understand how Rust's ownership rules help prevent memory leaks, ensure safe data access, and eliminate data races. Through examples, you saw how **ownership** works with variables, how **borrowing** allows you to safely access data without taking ownership, and how **references** are used to enable efficient memory management.

The concept of **lifetimes** was also covered, showing how Rust tracks the validity of references to ensure that you never access data after it has gone out of scope.

Finally, in the hands-on project, you applied these concepts by creating a function that manipulates a vector of strings, showcasing both ownership and borrowing in action. With this foundational understanding, you are well on your way to writing safe and efficient systems code in Rust.

Chapter 4: Rust Control Flow: Making Decisions and Loops

Overview: Covering Conditional Statements, Loops, and Pattern Matching

Control flow is a crucial aspect of programming, and Rust provides a set of powerful constructs to manage how your program makes decisions and repeats actions. In this chapter, we'll explore **conditional statements, loops,** and **pattern matching,** all of which allow you to control the execution of your Rust programs.

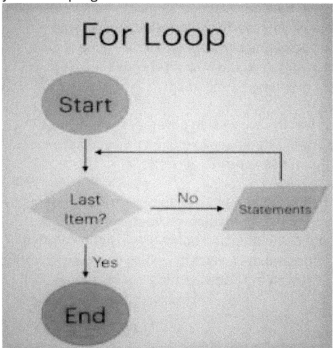

- **Conditional Statements**: These allow your program to make decisions based on certain conditions, executing different blocks of code based on whether a condition is true or false.
- **Loops**: Loops are used when you want to repeat actions multiple times. Rust provides several types of loops that give you fine control over how and when your code repeats.
- **Pattern Matching**: Rust's pattern matching feature is one of its standout features, allowing you to simplify complex conditional logic into clean and readable code.

In the hands-on project at the end of this chapter, we'll create a fun game called **"Guess the Number"** that combines these control flow techniques. You'll use conditional statements and loops to guide the flow of the game as the player guesses a random number.

If, Else, and Match Statements

Conditional statements are used to perform different actions based on whether a condition is true or false. Rust provides a few ways to work with conditional logic, including if, else, and match statements. Let's explore how to use them effectively.

1. The if Statement

The if statement allows you to execute code if a condition is true. It's the most basic form of decision-making in Rust. Here's a simple example:

```rust
fn main() {
```

```
    let number = 6;

    if number % 2 == 0 {
        println!("The number is even.");
    }
}
```

In this example, the program checks if `number` is divisible by 2 (i.e., if it's an even number). If the condition is true, it prints `"The number is even."`

You can also add an `else` block to handle cases where the condition is false:

rust

```
fn main() {
    let number = 7;

    if number % 2 == 0 {
        println!("The number is even.");
    } else {
        println!("The number is odd.");
    }
}
```

Here, if the number is not divisible by 2, it prints `"The number is odd."`

2. The `else if` Statement

You can chain multiple conditions together using `else if`. This is useful when you have several possible conditions to check, and each one requires a different action.

rust

```
fn main() {
    let number = 15;
```

```
    if number % 2 == 0 {
        println!("The number is even.");
    } else if number % 3 == 0 {
        println!("The number is divisible by 3.");
    } else {
        println!("The number is neither even nor
divisible by 3.");
    }
}
```

In this example, the program checks if the number is divisible by 2, then checks if it is divisible by 3. If neither condition is true, it falls back to the `else` block.

3. The `match` Statement

Rust's `match` statement is a powerful tool for handling multiple conditions in a more readable way. Instead of writing several `if` and `else if` statements, `match` allows you to cleanly match a value against different patterns. It is often compared to a switch statement in other languages, but it is more powerful due to Rust's pattern matching capabilities.

Here's an example of how to use `match`:

rust

```
fn main() {
    let number = 7;

    match number {
        1 => println!("One"),
        2 => println!("Two"),
        3 => println!("Three"),
        _ => println!("A different number"),
    }
}
```

In this case, `match` checks the value of `number` and compares it to the patterns (1, 2, and 3). If none of the patterns match, the wildcard _ is used, and it prints `"A different number"`.

You can also use more complex patterns in `match`:

rust

```
fn main() {
    let number = 15;

    match number {
        1 | 2 | 3 => println!("One, Two, or Three"),
        4..=10 => println!("A number between 4 and
10"),
        _ => println!("A different number"),
    }
}
```

Here, the first arm matches if the number is 1, 2, or 3. The second arm uses a range (`4..=10`) to match numbers between 4 and 10. The _ wildcard handles all other cases.

`match` is particularly useful when you need to handle different types of data or patterns, such as matching against enums or struct variants.

Loops: While, For, and Loop

Rust offers several ways to repeat actions in your programs, and each loop construct gives you different levels of control over how and when the loop executes.

1. The `while` Loop

The `while` loop repeats a block of code as long as a given condition is true. The condition is checked before each iteration, and if the condition is false at the start, the loop will not execute.

Here's an example of a `while` loop:

rust

```
fn main() {
    let mut counter = 0;

    while counter < 5 {
        println!("Counter: {}", counter);
        counter += 1;
    }
}
```

In this example, the loop continues as long as `counter` is less than 5. The value of `counter` is incremented on each iteration, and once the condition is false, the loop terminates.

2. The `for` Loop

Rust's `for` loop is one of the most commonly used loop types because of its flexibility and ease of use. It iterates over a range, collection, or iterator and executes a block of code for each element.

Here's an example using a range:

rust

```
fn main() {
    for i in 0..5 {
        println!("i: {}", i);
```

```
    }
}
```

The range `0..5` is an inclusive range, so it will loop from 0 to 4, printing the value of `i` at each iteration.

You can also iterate over collections like arrays or vectors:

rust

```
fn main() {
    let numbers = vec![10, 20, 30, 40];

    for number in numbers {
        println!("{}", number);
    }
}
```

In this case, the loop iterates over the `numbers` vector, printing each element.

3. The `loop`

The `loop` construct in Rust is an infinite loop that will continue until you explicitly break out of it. It's useful when you want to create a loop that runs indefinitely but needs to be stopped under certain conditions.

Here's an example:

rust

```
fn main() {
    let mut counter = 0;

    loop {
        counter += 1;
        println!("Counter: {}", counter);
```

```
        if counter == 5 {
            break;   // Exit the loop when counter
reaches 5
        }
    }
}
```

In this case, the loop will run indefinitely, but the `break` statement stops the loop once `counter` reaches 5.

Using Pattern Matching to Simplify Code

Pattern matching in Rust allows you to perform complex conditional logic in a clear, concise, and readable way. It can be used with `match` statements, `if let`, and `while let`. In many cases, pattern matching can simplify code that would otherwise require multiple `if` and `else` statements.

1. Pattern Matching with `match`

As we saw earlier, `match` is an incredibly powerful tool in Rust. It's especially useful when working with enums, structs, or any kind of data that can take multiple forms. Here's an example of pattern matching with an enum:

rust

```
enum Direction {
    Up,
    Down,
    Left,
    Right,
}

fn move_player(direction: Direction) {
    match direction {
        Direction::Up => println!("Moving up"),
```

```
        Direction::Down => println!("Moving down"),
        Direction::Left => println!("Moving left"),
        Direction::Right => println!("Moving right"),
    }
}
```

In this example, `move_player` takes a `Direction` enum and matches against each of its variants. This is much more concise than using multiple `if` or `else` statements.

2. Using `if let` for Simple Matching

Sometimes, you only need to match a single case of an enum or a value. In such cases, `if let` is more concise and efficient than `match`.

rust

```
enum Direction {
    Up,
    Down,
    Left,
    Right,
}

fn move_player(direction: Direction) {
    if let Direction::Up = direction {
        println!("Moving up");
    }
}
```

In this case, `if let` matches the `Direction::Up` variant. It's perfect for situations where you only care about one specific case and don't need to handle every possible variant.

Hands-on Project: Create a Game of "Guess the Number" Using Conditional Statements and Loops

Let's bring everything we've learned together in a fun hands-on project! We'll create a simple number guessing game where the program generates a random number, and the user has to guess it.

Step 1: Set Up the Project

Create a new project with Cargo:

```bash
cargo new guess_the_number
cd guess_the_number
```

Step 2: Write the Code

Now, let's write the game logic inside the `src/main.rs` file:

```rust
use std::io;
use rand::Rng;

fn main() {
    println!("Welcome to Guess the Number!");

    // Generate a random number between 1 and 100
    let secret_number =
rand::thread_rng().gen_range(1..=100);

    loop {
        println!("Please enter your guess:");

        let mut guess = String::new();
        io::stdin().read_line(&mut
guess).expect("Failed to read line");
```

```
let guess: u32 = match guess.trim().parse() {
    Ok(num) => num,
    Err(_) => {
        println!("Please enter a valid
number.");
        continue;
    }
};

if guess < secret_number {
    println!("Too low!");
} else if guess > secret_number {
    println!("Too high!");
} else {
    println!("You guessed it! The number was
{}.", secret_number);
    break;
}
    }
}
```

Step 3: Explanation

- We use `rand::Rng` to generate a random number between 1 and 100.
- We enter a `loop`, asking the user for input until they guess the correct number.
- The user's guess is matched against the secret number, and based on the comparison, they're told if their guess is too low, too high, or correct.

Step 4: Run the Program

To run the game, execute the following command:

```bash
cargo run
```

The game will continue prompting the user for guesses until the correct number is guessed.

Conclusion

In this chapter, you learned the basics of Rust's control flow constructs, including conditional statements (`if`, `else`, `match`), loops (`while`, `for`, and `loop`), and pattern matching. We also applied these concepts in a fun hands-on project where you created a number guessing game.

Mastering control flow is essential to writing effective Rust programs. As you continue to build your Rust skills, understanding these constructs will allow you to handle complex logic and build programs that can make decisions and repeat actions efficiently.

Chapter 5: Structs and Enums: Organizing Your Code

Overview: Learn How to Use Structs and Enums to Represent Complex Data Structures

As you advance in your Rust journey, you'll encounter scenarios where you need to represent more complex data. In Rust, two key constructs are used to model such data: **structs** and **enums**. These powerful tools allow you to create custom data types, organize your code, and manage multiple related values in a structured way.

- **Structs**: These are used to group multiple related values together into one cohesive unit. They allow you to create complex data structures that can hold different types of data, making your code more readable and maintainable.
- **Enums**: These are used to represent data that can take on a limited number of values, which is great for handling situations where you have a known set of possible options or states.

In this chapter, we'll dive deep into how to use **structs** to represent real-world objects and **enums** to model discrete values. We'll also look at how you can create methods and associated functions to add functionality to these types.

By the end of this chapter, you will have a clear understanding of how to organize your code using these types and apply them to real-world problems. We'll wrap up with a hands-on project where we build a **task management system** that uses structs to represent tasks and enums for task status.

What Are Structs and How to Use Them

In Rust, a **struct** is a custom data type that lets you group related data into one unit. A struct can contain fields of different types, and it helps you organize your data more logically. Imagine that you're building a system that manages different types of information, like users, tasks, and products—structs allow you to define how each of these should be structured.

1. Defining a Simple Struct

A basic struct in Rust is defined using the `struct` keyword followed by the name of the struct and its fields. Here's an example:

```rust
struct Person {
    name: String,
    age: u32,
}
```

In this example, `Person` is a struct with two fields: `name`, which is a `String`, and `age`, which is a `u32` (an unsigned 32-bit integer). This struct groups the person's name and age together in a single unit.

2. Creating an Instance of a Struct

Once you have defined a struct, you can create an instance of it and assign values to its fields:

rust

```
fn main() {
    let person = Person {
        name: String::from("Alice"),
        age: 30,
    };
    println!("Name: {}, Age: {}", person.name,
person.age);
}
```

In this code:

- We create an instance of Person called person.
- We assign values to the name and age fields.
- We print the values of these fields.

3. Updating Fields of a Struct

Once a struct is created, you can modify its fields if the struct is mutable:

rust

```
fn main() {
    let mut person = Person {
        name: String::from("Alice"),
        age: 30,
    };

    person.age = 31; // Mutating the age field
    println!("Updated Age: {}", person.age);
}
```

In this example:

- `person` is mutable (`let mut person`), so we can change its `age` field.
- We then print the updated age.

4. Using Structs with Functions

You can pass structs to functions, just like any other data type. By default, when you pass a struct to a function, its ownership is moved. If you want to **borrow** the struct, you can pass a reference instead:

rust

```
fn print_person_info(person: &Person) {
    println!("Name: {}, Age: {}", person.name,
person.age);
}

fn main() {
    let person = Person {
        name: String::from("Bob"),
        age: 25,
    };

    print_person_info(&person); // Borrowing the
reference
}
```

In this case, `print_person_info` takes an immutable reference (`&Person`) to the struct, so the ownership of the struct is not moved.

Enums: Handling Discrete Values in a Type-Safe Way

Enums are another powerful feature in Rust that allows you to define a type that can have several different, predefined values. Enums are useful when you want to represent a set of possible states or choices in your program, and you can be sure that the data will only take one of those values. In Rust, enums are more powerful than in many other languages, and they are widely used throughout the language's ecosystem.

1. Defining an Enum

To define an enum in Rust, you use the `enum` keyword, followed by the enum's name and the possible variants. Each variant can optionally have associated data.

Here's a simple example:

```rust
enum Direction {
    Up,
    Down,
    Left,
    Right,
}
```

In this example, `Direction` is an enum that represents four possible directions: `Up`, `Down`, `Left`, and `Right`. Each variant in this enum doesn't have any associated data, but you can add data to each variant if needed.

2. Using Enums with Data

Enums can also contain data for each of their variants. This allows you to store additional information that is related to the variant. Here's an example:

```rust
enum Shape {
    Circle(f64),          // Holds the radius of a circle
    Rectangle(f64, f64),  // Holds the width and height of a rectangle
    Square(f64),          // Holds the side length of a square
}
```

In this case:

- `Circle` holds a single `f64` value (the radius).
- `Rectangle` holds two `f64` values (the width and height).
- `Square` holds one `f64` value (the side length).

3. Using Enums in Code

Enums are typically used with `match` statements, which makes them very powerful for matching on different cases of an enum and handling each case appropriately.

Here's an example of how to use the `Shape` enum:

```rust
fn area(shape: Shape) -> f64 {
    match shape {
        Shape::Circle(radius) => std::f64::consts::PI * radius * radius,
```

```
        Shape::Rectangle(width, height) => width *
height,
        Shape::Square(side) => side * side,
    }
}

fn main() {
    let circle = Shape::Circle(10.0);
    let rectangle = Shape::Rectangle(5.0, 10.0);
    let square = Shape::Square(4.0);

    println!("Circle Area: {}", area(circle));
    println!("Rectangle Area: {}", area(rectangle));
    println!("Square Area: {}", area(square));
}
```

In this example, the `match` statement is used to handle the different variants of the `Shape` enum, and we calculate the area based on the type of shape.

4. Enums with Associated Functions

You can also define **methods** and **associated functions** for enums, just as you would for structs. Here's an example:

rust

```
impl Shape {
    fn describe(&self) {
        match *self {
            Shape::Circle(_) => println!("This is a
circle"),
            Shape::Rectangle(_, _) => println!("This
is a rectangle"),
            Shape::Square(_) => println!("This is a
square"),
        }
    }
}

fn main() {
```

```
    let shape = Shape::Circle(5.0);
    shape.describe();
}
```

In this example, the `describe` method is defined for the `Shape` enum, and it prints out a description based on the variant of the enum.

Methods and Associated Functions

Rust allows you to define both **methods** and **associated functions** on structs and enums. These allow you to encapsulate behavior within your data types, improving the organization and maintainability of your code.

1. Methods

A **method** is a function that is associated with a specific struct or enum. Methods are defined inside an `impl` block (short for "implementation block") and can take `self` as a parameter, which refers to the instance of the struct or enum.

Here's an example of a method for the `Person` struct:

rust

```
impl Person {
    fn greet(&self) {
        println!("Hello, {}!", self.name);
    }
}
```

In this code:

- The method `greet` is defined for `Person`.

- The `&self` parameter allows us to borrow the struct immutably.
- The method prints a greeting using the `name` field of the struct.

2. Associated Functions

An **associated function** is a function that is tied to a specific struct or enum but doesn't require an instance to be called. Associated functions are useful for things like constructors.

Here's an example of an associated function:

```rust
impl Person {
    fn new(name: String, age: u32) -> Person {
        Person { name, age }
    }
}
```

In this code:

- The `new` function is an associated function for creating a new `Person` instance.
- It takes a `name` and `age` as parameters and returns a new `Person` struct.

Hands-on Project: Build a Task Management System Using Structs and Enums

In this project, we'll build a **task management system** that uses structs and enums to represent tasks and their status. The goal is to create a simple system where you can track tasks, set their status, and update them as needed.

Step 1: Set Up the Project

Create a new project using Cargo:

```bash
bash
```

```bash
cargo new task_manager
cd task_manager
```

Step 2: Write the Code

In the `src/main.rs` file, define the following structs and enums:

```rust
rust

enum TaskStatus {
    Pending,
    InProgress,
    Completed,
}

struct Task {
    name: String,
    description: String,
    status: TaskStatus,
}

impl Task {
    fn new(name: &str, description: &str) -> Task {
        Task {
            name: name.to_string(),
            description: description.to_string(),
            status: TaskStatus::Pending,
        }
    }

    fn update_status(&mut self, status: TaskStatus) {
        self.status = status;
    }
```

```rust
    fn print_info(&self) {
        let status = match self.status {
            TaskStatus::Pending => "Pending",
            TaskStatus::InProgress => "In Progress",
            TaskStatus::Completed => "Completed",
        };
        println!("Task: {}\nDescription: {}\nStatus:
{}", self.name, self.description, status);
    }
}

fn main() {
    let mut task1 = Task::new("Finish Rust Chapter",
"Complete the Rust tutorial on structs and enums.");

    task1.print_info();

    task1.update_status(TaskStatus::InProgress);
    task1.print_info();

    task1.update_status(TaskStatus::Completed);
    task1.print_info();
}
```

Step 3: Explanation

Here's how the task management system works:

- **TaskStatus** is an enum that represents the three possible statuses of a task: `Pending`, `InProgress`, and `Completed`.
- **Task** is a struct that represents a task. It has three fields: `name`, `description`, and `status`.
- The `new` method is an associated function that creates a new `Task` with a default `Pending` status.
- The `update_status` method is a method that updates the task's status.
- The `print_info` method is a method that prints out the task's name, description, and status.

Step 4: Run the Program

Run the program with:

bash

```
cargo run
```

You should see the following output:

vbnet

```
Task: Finish Rust Chapter
Description: Complete the Rust tutorial on structs
and enums.
Status: Pending
Task: Finish Rust Chapter
Description: Complete the Rust tutorial on structs
and enums.
Status: In Progress
Task: Finish Rust Chapter
Description: Complete the Rust tutorial on structs
and enums.
Status: Completed
```

Conclusion

In this chapter, we explored two essential data structures in Rust: **structs** and **enums**. We learned how structs are used to group related data and how enums are used to represent a set of possible values. Additionally, we saw how methods and associated functions can be defined for both structs and enums, allowing us to encapsulate behavior and improve code organization.

Through the hands-on project, we built a **task management system** that used these concepts to model tasks and track their status. This system is just a starting point—you can extend it to include additional features, such as task prioritization, deadlines, and more.

With a solid understanding of structs, enums, and methods, you're now equipped to tackle more complex Rust projects.

Chapter 6: Error Handling in Rust: The Result and Option Types

Overview: Master Error Handling with Rust's Result and Option Types

Rust is a systems programming language designed to be safe and fast, and a large part of its safety comes from how it handles errors. Unlike many programming languages that rely on exceptions, Rust provides a robust, explicit way to handle errors using two powerful types: `Result` and `Option`. These types make error handling a first-class concept in Rust and help prevent many common bugs like null pointer exceptions, unchecked errors, and undefined behaviors that could otherwise lead to crashes or unexpected results in your applications.

In this chapter, we'll explore how Rust avoids exceptions and handles errors safely with `Result` and `Option` types. You'll learn how to use them effectively, understand their underlying principles, and leverage **pattern matching** to handle errors cleanly. We will also build a hands-on project where you implement a file reader that gracefully handles errors such as missing files or incorrect formats.

By the end of this chapter, you'll not only have a clear understanding of how error handling works in Rust, but you'll also be able to apply it confidently in real-world applications to ensure that your programs are both robust and reliable.

Why Rust Avoids Exceptions

Many programming languages rely on **exceptions** to handle errors. When an error occurs, the program throws an exception, which is then caught by the surrounding code to deal with it. While exceptions are useful for handling unexpected events, they have several downsides:

1. **Hidden errors**: Exceptions can propagate up the call stack and potentially be missed if not explicitly caught and handled. This means that errors can go unnoticed until they cause significant issues.
2. **Performance overhead**: Exceptions add performance overhead because they involve complex stack unwinding and memory management.
3. **Unclear flow of control**: Exception-based error handling can make it harder to follow the flow of the program, as control may jump unexpectedly.

Rust takes a different approach. Instead of using exceptions, Rust uses **types** (`Result` and `Option`) to handle errors explicitly. The key advantage of this is that error handling becomes part of the program's flow, and it is made clear what functions can fail and how errors will be handled. Rust's explicit error handling forces developers to think about failure paths and deal with them in a safe, predictable way.

By avoiding exceptions, Rust ensures that errors are handled directly and that the programmer has control over how and when the error is dealt with, making programs safer, easier to maintain, and less error-prone.

Using `Result` and `Option` for Safe Error Handling

Rust provides two primary types for handling errors: `Result` and `Option`. Both types are enums, and their usage depends on the kind of error you're dealing with. These types allow you to explicitly handle errors without relying on exceptions.

1. The `Result` Type

The `Result` type is used when a function can return a success or an error. It is defined as follows:

rust

```
enum Result<T, E> {
    Ok(T),
    Err(E),
}
```

- `T`: The type of the value returned in case of success.
- `E`: The type of the error in case of failure.

The `Ok` variant is used for success, and the `Err` variant is used for errors. You can think of `Result` as a way to explicitly handle both success and failure.

For example, consider a function that divides two numbers. In case of division by zero, the function will return an error:

rust

```
fn divide(a: f64, b: f64) -> Result<f64, String> {
    if b == 0.0 {
        Err(String::from("Cannot divide by zero"))
    } else {
        Ok(a / b)
    }
}
```

Here:

- If the division is successful, the function returns `Ok(a / b)`.
- If there's an error (e.g., division by zero), the function returns `Err("Cannot divide by zero")`.

The caller of this function is responsible for handling the result appropriately.

2. The `Option` Type

The **Option** type is used when there is a possibility that a value may be absent (i.e., the result is either **Some** or **None**). It's defined as follows:

rust

```
enum Option<T> {
    Some(T),
    None,
}
```

- **T**: The type of the value that is returned if the option is `Some`.
- **None**: Represents the absence of a value.

The `Option` type is particularly useful when you need to represent optional or missing data. For instance, if you try to find a value in a collection but it's not present, you can return an `Option`.

Here's an example:

rust

```
fn find_item(items: &[i32], target: i32) ->
Option<i32> {
    for &item in items {
        if item == target {
            return Some(item);
        }
    }
    None
}
```

In this example:

- If the `target` is found in the `items` slice, the function returns `Some(item)`.
- If the `target` is not found, the function returns `None`, indicating the absence of the value.

Pattern Matching with `Result` and `Option`

One of the most powerful features of Rust's error handling system is **pattern matching**. With pattern matching, you can easily handle different cases for both `Result` and `Option`. It allows you to write clean, efficient, and readable code when working with these types.

1. Pattern Matching with `Result`

When working with `Result`, you typically use pattern matching to handle the success and error cases separately. Here's an example:

```rust
fn main() {
    let result = divide(10.0, 2.0);
```

```
    match result {
        Ok(value) => println!("The result is {}",
value),
        Err(e) => println!("Error: {}", e),
    }
}
```

In this example:

- If the division is successful, the `Ok` variant is matched, and we print the result.
- If an error occurs (e.g., division by zero), the `Err` variant is matched, and we print the error message.

2. Pattern Matching with `Option`

Similarly, you can use pattern matching with `Option` to handle the `Some` and `None` cases:

rust

```
fn main() {
    let items = vec![1, 2, 3, 4, 5];
    let result = find_item(&items, 3);

    match result {
        Some(item) => println!("Found item: {}",
item),
        None => println!("Item not found"),
    }
}
```

In this example:

- If the item is found, the `Some(item)` variant is matched, and we print the found item.
- If the item is not found, the `None` variant is matched, and we print that the item is not found.

Hands-on Project: Implement a File Reader that Gracefully Handles Errors

Now that we understand how to use `Result` and `Option` for error handling, let's build a **file reader** that handles errors gracefully. This program will attempt to open a file, read its contents, and handle common errors like missing files or incorrect formats.

Step 1: Set Up the Project

Start by creating a new project:

bash

```
cargo new file_reader
cd file_reader
```

Step 2: Write the Code

Now, let's implement the file reader in the `src/main.rs` file:

rust

```
use std::fs::File;
use std::io::{self, Read};

fn read_file(filename: &str) -> Result<String,
String> {
    let mut file = File::open(filename).map_err(|_|
String::from("Failed to open file"))?;
    let mut contents = String::new();
    file.read_to_string(&mut contents).map_err(|_|
String::from("Failed to read file"))?;
    Ok(contents)
}

fn main() {
```

```
    let filename = "test.txt";

    match read_file(filename) {
        Ok(contents) => println!("File
contents:\n{}", contents),
        Err(e) => println!("Error: {}", e),
    }
}
```

Step 3: Explanation

Here's how the code works:

- The `read_file` function takes a filename and attempts to open the file.
- If opening the file fails, the `File::open` method returns a `Result` which is then matched using `.map_err()` to convert the error into a more user-friendly string.
- Once the file is opened, we attempt to read its contents using `read_to_string`. If reading fails, we again use `.map_err()` to handle the error.
- If everything goes well, the function returns an `Ok` with the file contents.
- The `main` function calls `read_file` and uses pattern matching to handle the `Ok` and `Err` cases, printing either the file contents or an error message.

Step 4: Create a Test File

For this program to work, you'll need to create a test file called `test.txt` in your project's directory. Add some simple text to the file, such as:

```kotlin

Hello, this is a test file.
Rust handles errors well!
```

Alternatively, if the file does not exist, the program should handle the error gracefully and print a user-friendly message.

Step 5: Run the Program

To run the program, use the following command:

```bash
cargo run
```

If the file `test.txt` exists, you should see the contents printed to the console. If the file does not exist, the program will print the error message `"Error: Failed to open file"`.

Conclusion

In this chapter, we've explored Rust's powerful error handling system, focusing on the `Result` and `Option` types. We learned how these types allow us to handle errors in a safe, explicit way, avoiding the pitfalls of exceptions. We also explored how to use **pattern matching** to handle different cases, making the code cleaner and more readable.

Finally, through the hands-on project, we implemented a **file reader** that handles errors like missing files and incorrect formats. By using `Result` and `Option`, we can ensure that our program handles errors gracefully, providing meaningful feedback to the user instead of crashing or behaving unpredictably.

Chapter 7: Collections in Rust: Vectors, Hash Maps, and Strings

Overview: Working with Rust's Built-in Collections for Handling Lists and Maps of Data

As you continue to build your knowledge of Rust, you'll encounter more complex data management needs. Whether you need to manage a list of items, a collection of key-value pairs, or manipulate text, Rust provides powerful built-in **collections** to help you store and organize data efficiently. Collections are a core part of programming, and Rust's collections are designed with performance and safety in mind.

In this chapter, we'll focus on three of Rust's most commonly used collections:

- **Vectors**: Dynamic arrays that allow you to store a collection of elements that can grow or shrink in size.
- **HashMaps**: A collection of key-value pairs that allows fast lookups and inserts based on keys.
- **Strings**: Rust offers two primary ways to handle text data: `String` and `&str`. Understanding the differences between them is key to working efficiently with text in Rust.

We'll also dive into **iterators** and **for loops**, which allow you to iterate over collections efficiently.

By the end of this chapter, you'll have a strong grasp of how to work with these collections and understand the powerful ways they can be used to solve real-world problems in Rust. We'll conclude with a **hands-on project**, where we will build a **contact book application** that stores and retrieves contacts using a `HashMap`.

Vectors and HashMaps in Rust

Rust provides collections that make it easy to work with lists, maps, and other types of data. Let's take a closer look at **vectors** and **hash maps**, two of the most common collections in Rust.

1. Vectors in Rust

A **vector** in Rust is a dynamically sized array. Unlike arrays, which have a fixed size, vectors allow you to add and remove elements dynamically. Vectors are particularly useful when you need a collection where the number of elements may change over time.

A vector is created using the `Vec` type in Rust. Here's how you can create and use vectors:

Creating a Vector:

To create an empty vector:

```rust
let mut v: Vec<i32> = Vec::new();
```

This creates an empty vector of integers (`i32`). You can also create a vector and initialize it with some values:

```rust
```

```rust
let v = vec![1, 2, 3, 4, 5];
```

Here, `vec!` is a macro that creates a new vector with the values provided inside the square brackets.

Adding Elements to a Vector:

You can add elements to a vector using the `push` method:

rust

```rust
let mut v = vec![1, 2, 3];
v.push(4);  // Adds 4 to the end of the vector
```

Accessing Elements in a Vector:

You can access elements in a vector by their index, similar to arrays:

rust

```rust
let v = vec![1, 2, 3];
println!("The first element is: {}", v[0]);
```

However, be careful—accessing an element with an invalid index will cause a panic. If you're not sure whether an index exists, you can use the `get` method, which returns an `Option`:

rust

```rust
let v = vec![1, 2, 3];
match v.get(2) {
    Some(&val) => println!("Found: {}", val),
    None => println!("Index out of bounds"),
}
```

This way, if the index is out of bounds, the program handles the error gracefully instead of panicking.

Iterating Over a Vector:

You can iterate over a vector using a `for` loop or an iterator:

```rust
let v = vec![1, 2, 3, 4, 5];
for val in &v {
    println!("{}", val);
}
```

This creates an immutable reference to each element in the vector and prints each one.

Modifying Elements in a Vector:

To modify an element, you can either access it by index (if the vector is mutable) or iterate with mutable references:

```rust
let mut v = vec![1, 2, 3, 4];
v[0] = 10;   // Direct modification by index

for val in &mut v {
    *val += 1;   // Increment each value by 1
}
```

In this example, the first element of the vector is changed to `10`, and then all elements are incremented by `1`.

2. Hash Maps in Rust

A **hash map** is a collection of key-value pairs, where each key maps to a specific value. Hash maps are incredibly efficient for lookups, as the key is hashed to quickly find its corresponding value. Rust's standard library provides the `HashMap` type, which is part of the `std::collections` module.

Here's how to create and use a hash map in Rust:

Creating a HashMap:

```rust
use std::collections::HashMap;

let mut map = HashMap::new();
```

This creates an empty hash map where both keys and values are of type `i32`. You can insert values into the map with the `insert` method:

```rust
map.insert(1, "one");
map.insert(2, "two");
map.insert(3, "three");
```

This inserts three key-value pairs into the map.

Accessing Values in a HashMap:

You can retrieve values from the hash map by using the key:

```rust
match map.get(&2) {
    Some(&val) => println!("Found: {}", val),
    None => println!("Key not found"),
}
```

In this case, `map.get(&2)` retrieves the value associated with key 2. If the key is found, it returns the value; otherwise, it returns `None`.

Iterating Over a HashMap:

You can iterate over a hash map using a `for` loop:

rust

```
for (key, value) in &map {
    println!("Key: {}, Value: {}", key, value);
}
```

This prints each key-value pair in the map.

Modifying Values in a HashMap:

You can update a value in a hash map by inserting a new value for an existing key:

rust

```
map.insert(1, "uno");
```

This updates the value for key 1 to `"uno"`.

You can also use `entry` API to modify a value only if the key exists or insert a default value if it does not:

rust

```
map.entry(2).or_insert("two_default");
```

If the key 2 already exists, this will leave the value unchanged. If the key does not exist, it inserts `"two_default"` as the value.

Handling Strings: `String` and `&str`

Rust handles strings differently than many other programming languages. It provides two primary types for dealing with text: `String` and `&str`. Understanding the differences between these types is crucial for managing string data efficiently.

1. `String` Type

The `String` type is an owned, growable string type. It is allocated on the heap and can be modified. You create a `String` by using the `String::from` method or the `to_string` method:

```rust
rust
```

```rust
let s = String::from("Hello");
let s2 = "World".to_string();
```

The `String` type is mutable, which means you can modify the contents:

```rust
rust
```

```rust
let mut s = String::from("Hello");
s.push_str(", world!"); // Appending to a String
println!("{}", s); // Output: Hello, world!
```

In this example, we create a `String` and append another string to it using `push_str`.

2. `&str` Type

The **`&str`** type is a reference to a string slice, and it is typically used to represent an immutable view of a string. It is often seen in function signatures or when working with string literals:

rust

```
let s: &str = "Hello, world!";
```

A string slice (`&str`) is a view of a string without ownership. It points to a portion of a `String` or a string literal. String slices are efficient because they don't involve ing the data—they simply borrow a part of the string.

3. Converting Between `String` and `&str`

You can convert between `String` and `&str` easily:

- To get a `&str` from a `String`, you can use `&` (a reference):

rust

```
let s = String::from("Hello");
let slice: &str = &s;
```

- To convert a `&str` to a `String`, you can call `to_string()` or `String::from()`:

rust

```
let slice: &str = "Hello";
let s = slice.to_string(); // or String::from(slice)
```

Iterators and For Loops with Collections

Rust's collections, like `Vec` and `HashMap`, are designed to work with **iterators**. Iterators allow you to process each element of a collection without manually managing the index or keys. Rust's iterator pattern is very powerful and allows for lazy evaluation, which can improve performance.

1. Using Iterators

You can create an iterator over a collection by calling the `iter()` method on a collection. For example:

rust

```
let v = vec![1, 2, 3, 4, 5];
let sum: i32 = v.iter().sum();
println!("The sum is: {}", sum);
```

In this case, `iter()` creates an iterator over the vector `v`, and `sum()` consumes the iterator to calculate the sum of the values.

2. Using `for` Loops with Iterators

Rust's `for` loops work seamlessly with iterators. When you use a `for` loop with a collection, it automatically converts the collection into an iterator. Here's an example:

rust

```
let v = vec![1, 2, 3, 4, 5];
for value in v {
    println!("{}", value);
}
```

In this case, the `for` loop automatically creates an iterator over `v` and iterates over each element.

3. Chaining Iterators

You can chain iterators to perform multiple actions on a collection. For example, you can filter, map, and collect the results:

```rust
let v = vec![1, 2, 3, 4, 5];
let even_squares: Vec<i32> = v.iter()
    .filter(|&&x| x % 2 == 0)
    .map(|&x| x * x)
    .collect();

println!("{:?}", even_squares); // Output: [4, 16]
```

In this example, we:

- Filter the vector to include only even numbers.
- Map each even number to its square.
- Collect the results into a new `Vec`.

Hands-on Project: Build a Contact Book Application that Stores and Retrieves Contacts Using a `HashMap`

Now that you've learned how to use Rust's collections, let's build a simple **contact book** application that stores and retrieves contacts using a `HashMap`. The contact book will allow us to store contacts with a name and phone number and then retrieve them by their name.

Step 1: Set Up the Project

Create a new project:

```bash
cargo new contact_book
cd contact_book
```

Step 2: Write the Code

Let's define the structure of a contact and implement a contact book using a HashMap.

```rust
use std::collections::HashMap;

#[derive(Debug)]
struct Contact {
    name: String,
    phone_number: String,
}

impl Contact {
    fn new(name: &str, phone_number: &str) -> Contact {
        Contact {
            name: name.to_string(),
            phone_number: phone_number.to_string(),
        }
    }
}

fn main() {
    let mut contact_book: HashMap<String, Contact> =
HashMap::new();

    // Adding contacts
    let contact1 = Contact::new("Alice", "123-456-
7890");
    let contact2 = Contact::new("Bob", "987-654-
3210");
```

```
    contact_book.insert(contact1.name.clone(),
contact1);
    contact_book.insert(contact2.name.clone(),
contact2);

    // Retrieving a contact
    let name = "Alice";
    match contact_book.get(name) {
        Some(contact) => println!("Contact found:
{:?}", contact),
        None => println!("Contact not found"),
    }

    // Displaying all contacts
    for (name, contact) in &contact_book {
        println!("{}: {:?}", name, contact);
    }
}
```

Step 3: Explanation

In this code:

- The `Contact` struct stores the name and phone number of a contact.
- The `Contact::new()` method is used to create new instances of the `Contact` struct.
- We use a `HashMap<String, Contact>` to store contacts by their name.
- We insert two contacts, `Alice` and `Bob`, into the hash map.
- We then retrieve `Alice` by name using the `get` method and display the contact's information.
- Finally, we iterate through all contacts in the contact book and print each one.

Step 4: Run the Program

To run the program, use the following command:

```bash
```

```
cargo run
```

The output will display the information for the contact named "Alice" if it exists, and then it will list all contacts in the contact book.

Conclusion

In this chapter, we've covered how to work with three essential Rust collections: **vectors**, **hash maps**, and **strings**. We learned how vectors provide dynamic arrays that can grow and shrink, how hash maps allow fast lookups with keys, and how Rust handles strings with `String` and `&str`. We also explored iterators and how to use `for` loops to efficiently iterate over collections.

In the hands-on project, we built a **contact book application** that used a `HashMap` to store and retrieve contacts. This project demonstrated how powerful and flexible Rust's collections can be in real-world applications.

With a solid understanding of these collections, you're now ready to tackle more complex problems involving data management and manipulation.

Chapter 8: Concurrency in Rust: Handling Multiple Threads

Overview: Rust's Approach to Safe Concurrency Using Threads

Concurrency allows a program to perform multiple tasks at the same time, making it a powerful tool for speeding up applications, especially in multi-core systems. Rust takes a unique approach to concurrency by making it **safe** and **efficient**. Unlike other programming languages that require complex, error-prone manual memory management, Rust's strict ownership model ensures that concurrency does not introduce issues like **data races**, **deadlocks**, or **race conditions**.

In this chapter, we will explore how Rust handles concurrency, focusing on **threads**, **mutexes**, and **channels**. These tools provide a way to split your program into multiple independent tasks that can run concurrently without violating Rust's memory safety guarantees.

We will also look at **asynchronous programming**, a model that allows tasks to run concurrently without using multiple threads. Finally, you will implement a **multithreaded program** to download multiple web pages simultaneously, demonstrating how these concepts work in practice.

How Rust's Ownership Model Helps Avoid Data Races

Rust's approach to concurrency is heavily influenced by its **ownership** and **borrowing** system, which enforces strict rules on how memory is accessed. These rules ensure that data races—an issue where multiple threads simultaneously access shared memory in conflicting ways—are virtually impossible in safe Rust code.

Data races happen when two or more threads access the same data at the same time, with at least one of them modifying the data. In languages without proper memory safety guarantees, data races can lead to unpredictable behavior, crashes, and hard-to-diagnose bugs. Rust prevents these issues by using its **ownership** model, which ensures that only one thread can modify data at a time.

Rust enforces this with the following rules:

1. **Ownership**: Only one thread can own a piece of data at a time. Once a thread takes ownership, no other thread can access that data unless it is explicitly shared (via borrowing).
2. **Borrowing**: Rust allows **immutable** borrowing, where multiple threads can read data simultaneously, but not **mutable** borrowing, where only one thread can modify the data at a time.
3. **Lifetimes**: Rust tracks how long a piece of data is valid (through lifetimes), ensuring that no thread uses data that has already been freed or is currently being modified by another thread.

These principles make it much easier to write safe, concurrent code that avoids data races without needing complex synchronization mechanisms. While Rust allows multiple threads to run simultaneously, it ensures that the memory access model prevents conflicts through ownership rules.

Using Threads, Mutexes, and Channels

Rust provides several powerful tools for working with concurrency: **threads**, **mutexes**, and **channels**. These tools let you split your program into multiple independent tasks that can run concurrently without risking memory safety violations.

1. Using Threads

Threads in Rust are created using the `std::thread` module. A thread is essentially a way to run a function concurrently with the main program. Each thread has its own stack, and threads can share data using channels or other synchronization mechanisms.

Here's a simple example of how to create a thread in Rust:

```rust
use std::thread;

fn main() {
    let handle = thread::spawn(|| {
        println!("Hello from a thread!");
    });

    handle.join().unwrap(); // Wait for the thread to finish
}
```

In this example:

- We create a new thread using `thread::spawn`, passing a closure that defines the work the thread will do.
- `handle.join()` waits for the thread to finish before continuing with the rest of the program. This is a blocking call, meaning the main thread will wait for the spawned thread to complete before it proceeds.

You can spawn multiple threads and have them run concurrently. However, as we discussed earlier, Rust's ownership system ensures that these threads will not have conflicts over shared data unless we use safe mechanisms like `Mutexes` or `Channels`.

2. Using Mutexes for Shared Mutable Data

When multiple threads need to access and modify the same data, we need to use a **mutex** (short for mutual exclusion), which is a synchronization primitive that ensures only one thread can access the data at a time.

Rust provides a `Mutex` type in the `std::sync` module to achieve this. The `Mutex` guarantees that only one thread can access the data inside the mutex at any given time. If another thread tries to access the data while it's locked, it will be forced to wait.

Here's an example of using a `Mutex` to safely share mutable data between threads:

```rust
use std::sync::{Arc, Mutex};
use std::thread;

fn main() {
    let counter = Arc::new(Mutex::new(0)); // `Arc`
makes it shareable between threads
```

```
    let mut handles = vec![];

    for _ in 0..10 {
        let counter = Arc::clone(&counter);

        let handle = thread::spawn(move || {
            let mut num = counter.lock().unwrap(); //
Lock the mutex
            *num += 1; // Modify the value
        });

        handles.push(handle);
    }

    for handle in handles {
        handle.join().unwrap(); // Wait for all
threads to finish
    }

    println!("Result: {}", *counter.lock().unwrap());
// Print the final result
}
```

In this example:

- We use an `Arc` (atomic reference counter) to allow multiple threads to safely share ownership of the `Mutex`.
- Each thread locks the mutex before modifying the shared `counter` variable.
- The `lock()` method locks the mutex and returns a guard that allows safe access to the data. The guard is automatically released when it goes out of scope.

The `Mutex` ensures that only one thread can modify the `counter` at a time, preventing data races and ensuring safe concurrent access.

3. Using Channels for Communication Between Threads

Sometimes, threads need to communicate with each other. Rust's `std::sync::mpsc` module provides **channels** for message passing. A channel allows one thread to send data to another, and it works like a mailbox: one thread sends a message, and another thread receives it.

Here's an example of using channels to send data between threads:

rust

```
use std::sync::mpsc;
use std::thread;

fn main() {
    let (tx, rx) = mpsc::channel(); // Create a
channel with a transmitter and receiver

    thread::spawn(move || {
        let val = String::from("Hello from the
thread!");
        tx.send(val).unwrap(); // Send a message
through the channel
    });

    let received = rx.recv().unwrap(); // Receive the
message
    println!("Received: {}", received);
}
```

In this example:

- We create a channel with `mpsc::channel()`, which returns a transmitter (`tx`) and a receiver (`rx`).
- The thread sends a message (`val`) through the transmitter, and the main thread receives it using the receiver (`rx`).

- `recv()` blocks until a message is received, so the main thread waits for the message from the spawned thread.

Channels are a great way to share data safely between threads because they enforce a message-passing model, eliminating the need for shared memory access.

The Future of Concurrency: Async Programming in Rust

While threads and synchronization primitives like mutexes and channels are effective for many types of concurrency, Rust also offers **asynchronous programming** (async/await) to handle concurrent tasks more efficiently. Asynchronous programming allows your program to handle many tasks concurrently without blocking threads, making it ideal for I/O-bound tasks like web requests, file operations, and networking.

Rust introduced asynchronous programming with the `async` and `await` keywords in version 1.39. With async programming, tasks can run concurrently on a single thread, which can greatly improve efficiency when you have many I/O-bound operations that don't require heavy computation.

Here's a basic example of using async functions in Rust:

```rust
use tokio; // A popular async runtime for Rust

#[tokio::main]
async fn main() {
    let result = fetch_data().await;
    println!("Fetched data: {}", result);
}
```

```
async fn fetch_data() -> String {
    // Simulating an async operation, e.g., an HTTP
request
    "Some data".to_string()
}
```

In this example:

- We use `#[tokio::main]` to set up the async runtime.
- `fetch_data` is an async function that simulates fetching data asynchronously.
- The `await` keyword is used to wait for the result of an asynchronous operation.

Rust's async model allows you to run many tasks concurrently without spawning multiple threads, reducing the overhead associated with thread management. This is particularly useful for tasks like web servers, where multiple clients need to be handled concurrently without blocking the main thread.

Hands-on Project: Implement a Multithreaded Program That Downloads Multiple Web Pages Simultaneously

Now that you understand the basics of concurrency in Rust, let's build a hands-on project to download multiple web pages concurrently using threads. We'll use Rust's thread management features, along with `reqwest` (an HTTP client library), to download web pages in parallel.

Step 1: Set Up the Project

Create a new project:

```
bash
```

```
cargo new web_downloader
cd web_downloader
```

Add the `reqwest` dependency to your `Cargo.toml` file:

```
toml

[dependencies]
reqwest = "0.11"
tokio = { version = "1", features = ["full"] }
```

Step 2: Write the Code

In the `src/main.rs` file, implement the multithreaded web downloader:

```rust
rust

use reqwest;
use std::thread;

async fn download_page(url: &str) -> String {
    let response = reqwest::get(url).await.unwrap();
    response.text().await.unwrap()
}

fn main() {
    let urls = vec![
        "https://www.rust-lang.org",
        "https://www.wikipedia.org",
        "https://www.github.com",
    ];

    let mut handles = vec![];

    for url in urls {
        let handle = thread::spawn(move || {
            let result =
tokio::runtime::Runtime::new()
                .unwrap()
                .block_on(download_page(url));
```

```
            println!("Downloaded content from: {}",
url);
            println!("{}", result);
        });

        handles.push(handle);
    }

    for handle in handles {
        handle.join().unwrap();
    }
}
```

Step 3: Explanation

In this program:

- We define an async function `download_page` that downloads the content of a URL using `reqwest`.
- In the `main` function, we create a list of URLs to download.
- We spawn a new thread for each URL and use `tokio::runtime::Runtime::new().unwrap().block_on()` to run the asynchronous `download_page` function within each thread.
- Each thread waits for the result and prints the downloaded content.

Step 4: Run the Program

To run the program, use:

```bash
cargo run
```

You should see the content of the downloaded web pages printed to the console.

Conclusion

In this chapter, we explored Rust's approach to concurrency, focusing on **threads**, **mutexes**, **channels**, and **asynchronous programming**. Rust's ownership and borrowing model ensures that concurrent programming is safe and free from data races, while tools like threads and channels allow you to build powerful, concurrent applications.

We also covered **async programming**, which allows for efficient concurrency without using multiple threads, and we implemented a **multithreaded web downloader** as a hands-on project, showcasing how to download multiple web pages simultaneously using threads.

Chapter 9: Rust's Cargo: The Rust Package Manager

Overview: Learn How to Use Cargo to Manage Dependencies, Build, and Run Rust Projects

When working with Rust, **Cargo** is your best friend. It's the official package manager and build system for Rust, and it handles much of the hard work for you. Cargo takes care of managing dependencies, compiling code, running tests, building projects, and even packaging your code for distribution. Whether you're starting a small project or building something larger, Cargo simplifies a lot of the repetitive tasks that would otherwise slow you down.

In this chapter, we'll dive deep into Cargo's features, learning how to create projects, manage dependencies, and run tests using this essential tool. Cargo is what allows developers to focus on writing code rather than managing files or manually handling configurations. We'll also walk through the process of creating a command-line interface (CLI) tool that takes user input and executes different operations based on commands.

By the end of this chapter, you will have a solid understanding of how to use Cargo effectively, and you'll be able to apply it to organize, build, and test your Rust projects.

Creating Projects with Cargo

Cargo makes it incredibly easy to create, organize, and manage Rust projects. Whether you're starting from scratch or building on an existing project, Cargo can handle the setup with just a few commands.

1. Creating a New Project

To create a new Rust project with Cargo, you use the `cargo new` command, followed by the name of your project. This will generate a new directory with the necessary files for a Rust project.

For example, let's create a new project called `hello_world`:

bash

```
cargo new hello_world
```

This will create a new directory called `hello_world`, and inside this directory, Cargo will generate the following files:

- `Cargo.toml`: This is the configuration file for the project, where dependencies and metadata about the project are stored.
- `src/main.rs`: This is the default entry point for a Rust application. It contains the `main` function that gets executed when the program runs.

You can change into the new project directory with:

bash

```
cd hello_world
```

Now you're ready to build and run the project.

2. Understanding the `Cargo.toml` File

The `Cargo.toml` file is the manifest of your Rust project. It's where you define the project metadata, dependencies, and configuration. Here's what the `Cargo.toml` file might look like for the `hello_world` project:

```toml
[package]
name = "hello_world"
version = "0.1.0"
edition = "2018"

[dependencies]
```

The `[package]` section defines metadata about the project:

- **name**: The name of the package (your project).
- **version**: The version number of the project.
- **edition**: The Rust edition to use (Rust 2018 edition is the default).

The `[dependencies]` section is where you list any external crates (libraries) that your project depends on. Since this is a new project with no dependencies, this section is currently empty.

3. Running Your Project

To run your project, simply use the following command:

```bash
cargo run
```

This command does two things:

1. It **compiles** your code (if needed).
2. It **runs** the compiled binary.

If you look inside the `src/main.rs` file, you'll see the default "Hello, world!" program:

```rust
fn main() {
    println!("Hello, world!");
}
```

Running `cargo run` will display:

```
Hello, world!
```

Managing Dependencies with Cargo.toml

In most projects, you'll need to use external libraries (also known as **crates**) to extend the functionality of your program. Cargo makes it easy to manage dependencies through the `Cargo.toml` file. This file tracks all external dependencies, along with their versions, to ensure your project is built consistently across different environments.

1. Adding Dependencies

To add a dependency to your project, you simply need to modify the `[dependencies]` section of the `Cargo.toml` file. For example, let's say we want to add the popular `serde` crate, which is used for serializing and deserializing data:

```toml
```

```
[dependencies]
serde = "1.0"
```

Once the dependency is added to `Cargo.toml`, you can use it in your code. Cargo will automatically download and compile the `serde` crate the next time you build your project.

To include a dependency in your Rust code, you use the `use` keyword, like this:

```
rust
```

```
use serde::{Serialize, Deserialize};
```

2. Updating Dependencies

When dependencies are added or updated in the `Cargo.toml` file, Cargo can fetch and compile them using the `cargo build` command. This ensures that your project is always using the correct versions of the libraries.

To update all dependencies to their latest compatible versions based on your `Cargo.toml`, run:

```
bash
```

```
cargo update
```

This will update the `Cargo.lock` file, which locks the specific versions of dependencies your project is using.

3. Specifying Dependency Versions

Cargo allows you to specify versions of dependencies using version ranges. This flexibility helps you ensure compatibility while still taking advantage of newer versions of libraries. Here's how you can specify different version ranges:

- **Exact version**: To use a specific version, specify it directly:

```toml
[dependencies]
serde = "=1.0.130"
```

- **Compatible version**: To use any version that is compatible with a given version, use a caret (^):

```toml
[dependencies]
serde = "^1.0"
```

- **Minimum version**: To use a minimum version but allow any higher version:

```toml
[dependencies]
serde = ">=1.0"
```

Cargo handles version resolution automatically, ensuring that your dependencies are compatible with each other.

Building and Testing with Cargo

Cargo not only helps you manage dependencies but also makes building and testing your Rust code straightforward. Let's explore how to build and test your projects using Cargo.

1. Building Your Project

To compile your project and produce the final executable, you can use the `cargo build` command:

bash

```
cargo build
```

This will compile your project and place the output binary in the `target/debug` directory. You can then run the binary manually:

bash

```
./target/debug/hello_world
```

If you want to build your project in release mode (optimized for performance), use the `--release` flag:

bash

```
cargo build --release
```

This will compile the project with optimizations, and the output binary will be placed in the `target/release` directory.

2. Running Tests with Cargo

Cargo makes testing in Rust simple with its built-in test framework. To write a test, simply create functions inside a module annotated with `#[cfg(test)]`. These functions should have the `#[test]` attribute.

Here's an example of a test in Rust:

rust

```
#[cfg(test)]
mod tests {
    #[test]
    fn test_addition() {
        assert_eq!(2 + 2, 4);
    }
}
```

This test checks that `2 + 2` equals `4`. You can run all tests in your project with the following command:

```bash
cargo test
```

This will run any function marked with `#[test]` and report the results. If a test fails, Cargo will display an error message with information about the failure.

3. Testing with Assertions

Rust's test framework includes a number of useful assertions to help check that your code is working as expected:

- `assert_eq!(a, b)` checks that `a` equals `b`.
- `assert_ne!(a, b)` checks that `a` does not equal `b`.
- `assert!(condition)` checks that the condition is true.
- `assert!(!condition)` checks that the condition is false.

Here's an example using assertions:

```rust
#[cfg(test)]
mod tests {
    #[test]
```

```
fn test_multiplication() {
    assert_eq!(2 * 3, 6);
}

#[test]
fn test_subtraction() {
    assert!(5 - 3 == 2);
}
}
```

If all the tests pass, you'll see a success message. If any test fails, Cargo will show a detailed error message to help you diagnose the issue.

Hands-on Project: Create a CLI Tool That Takes User Input and Runs Different Operations Based on Commands

Now that you have a solid understanding of how Cargo works and how to manage projects and dependencies, let's build a practical command-line interface (CLI) tool. This tool will take user input and execute different operations based on the commands entered.

In this project, we will:

- Accept user input through the command line.
- Parse the input and perform operations like addition, subtraction, and multiplication.
- Organize the tool's functionality into separate commands using Cargo's tools and external crates.

Step 1: Set Up the Project

Create a new Cargo project:

```bash
cargo new cli_tool
cd cli_tool
```

Step 2: Add Dependencies

We will use the `clap` crate, which is a popular library for parsing command-line arguments in Rust. Add it to the `[dependencies]` section of your `Cargo.toml` file:

```toml
[dependencies]
clap = "3.0"
```

Step 3: Write the Code

In the `src/main.rs` file, write the following code to implement the CLI tool:

```rust
use clap::{App, Arg};

fn main() {
    let matches = App::new("Simple Calculator")
        .version("1.0")
        .author("Rust Developer")
        .about("Performs basic arithmetic
operations")
        .arg(Arg::new("operation")
            .short('o')
            .long("operation")
            .takes_value(true)
            .help("Specifies the operation to perform
(add, subtract, multiply)"))
        .arg(Arg::new("num1")
            .short('a')
            .long("num1")
            .takes_value(true)
```

```
            .help("First number"))
        .arg(Arg::new("num2")
            .short('b')
            .long("num2")
            .takes_value(true)
            .help("Second number"))
        .get_matches();

    let operation =
matches.value_of("operation").unwrap_or("add");
    let num1: f64 =
matches.value_of("num1").unwrap_or("0").parse().unwra
p();
    let num2: f64 =
matches.value_of("num2").unwrap_or("0").parse().unwra
p();

    let result = match operation {
        "add" => num1 + num2,
        "subtract" => num1 - num2,
        "multiply" => num1 * num2,
        _ => {
            println!("Unknown operation: {}",
operation);
            return;
        }
    };

    println!("Result: {}", result);
}
```

Step 4: Explanation

In this code:

- We use the `clap` crate to parse the command-line arguments. The `operation` argument specifies the operation to perform, and the `num1` and `num2` arguments specify the numbers to use in the operation.
- The `match` statement checks which operation the user wants to perform and executes the corresponding

arithmetic operation (addition, subtraction, or multiplication).
- If the operation is not recognized, the program prints an error message.

Step 5: Run the Program

To build and run the CLI tool, use the following commands:

```bash
cargo build
cargo run -- --operation add --num1 5 --num2 3
```

This will output:

```makefile
Result: 8
```

You can change the operation and numbers to test other functionality:

```bash
cargo run -- --operation subtract --num1 5 --num2 3
cargo run -- --operation multiply --num1 5 --num2 3
```

Conclusion

In this chapter, we've explored how to use **Cargo** to manage Rust projects, handle dependencies, build and test code, and more. We covered the core features of Cargo, including how to create projects, add dependencies, and compile and run your code.

We also built a practical hands-on project: a **CLI tool** that takes user input and performs arithmetic operations based on the command-line arguments. This tool demonstrated how to work with external crates like `clap` and how Cargo makes it easy to manage and run Rust projects.

Chapter 10: Rust for Web Development: Using Rocket for Building Web Apps

---

Overview: Introduction to Building Web Applications with Rust

Rust is well-known for its performance, reliability, and safety, but did you know it can also be used for building web applications? While Rust may not have the same number of web development frameworks as languages like JavaScript or Python, it has a rising ecosystem of tools that make it a strong candidate for web development.

In this chapter, we'll dive into building web applications using **Rocket**, one of the most popular web frameworks in Rust. Rocket is fast, secure, and designed to be easy to use, which makes it a great choice for anyone looking to build web applications in Rust.

We'll start with the basics: setting up Rocket, creating simple routes, and handling requests and responses. Then, we'll get into more advanced topics such as form handling, templates, and building a complete CRUD (Create, Read, Update, Delete) application. By the end of this chapter, you'll be able to build powerful web applications with Rocket, taking full advantage of Rust's performance and safety features.

Setting Up Rocket for Web Development

Before we can dive into web development with Rocket, we need to get our environment set up. Luckily, setting up Rocket is fairly straightforward. Let's walk through the steps to get Rocket installed and create our first project.

1. Installing Rocket

Rocket requires a few dependencies to run, and we'll need to add them to our `Cargo.toml` file. You'll need the `rocket` crate and the `tokio` runtime to handle asynchronous tasks (since Rocket uses async Rust under the hood).

Here's how to get started:

1. Create a new Rust project using Cargo:

bash

```
cargo new rocket_app
cd rocket_app
```

2. Open the `Cargo.toml` file and add Rocket as a dependency:

toml

```
[dependencies]
rocket = "0.5.0-rc.2"
tokio = { version = "1", features = ["full"] }
```

In this example:

- **rocket = "0.5.0-rc.2"** specifies the version of Rocket. At the time of writing, Rocket is in release candidate 2 for version 0.5, but you should always check for the latest stable version.

- **tokio** is required because Rocket depends on the async runtime for handling concurrent operations. The features = ["full"] line ensures that all necessary features are enabled.

3. Next, in the src/main.rs file, import Rocket and create a basic "Hello, World!" application:

```rust
#[macro_use] extern crate rocket;

#[launch]
fn rocket() -> _ {
    rocket::build().mount("/", routes![index])
}

#[get("/")]
fn index() -> &'static str {
    "Hello, world!"
}
```

In this example:

- **#[macro_use] extern crate rocket;** imports Rocket's macros, which we'll use to define routes and other aspects of the web app.
- The rocket() function is the entry point to our application. The #[launch] macro tells Rocket to launch the server when the program starts.
- **mount("/", routes![index])** mounts the index route to the root URL (/). This is where the server will listen for requests.

- `#[get("/")]` is a Rocket attribute macro that defines the `index` route for GET requests to `/`. It returns a static string, `"Hello, world!"`.

2. Running the Application

To run your Rocket application, use the following command:

```bash
cargo run
```

This will compile the application and start a server on `localhost:8000`. You should see the following output:

```javascript
🚀 Rocket has launched from 'target/debug/rocket_app'
as 'rocket_app'
    :: Running on http://localhost:8000
```

You can visit `http://localhost:8000` in your browser, and you should see the "Hello, world!" message.

Basic Routing, Handling Requests and Responses

Now that we have our Rocket application set up, let's take a deeper look at **routing, handling requests**, and **returning responses**.

1. Defining Routes in Rocket

In Rocket, routes are defined using attribute macros like `#[get("/")]` for GET requests, `#[post("/")]` for POST requests, and other HTTP methods such as PUT, DELETE, PATCH, etc.

Here's how you can define a POST route:

rust

```
#[post("/submit", data = "<name>")]
fn submit(name: String) -> String {
    format!("Received name: {}", name)
}
```

- The `#[post("/submit")]` macro defines a route for handling POST requests to `/submit`.
- `data = "<name>"` tells Rocket to parse the incoming request body as a `String` and pass it to the `submit` function.
- The `submit` function returns a formatted string with the submitted name.

2. Request Parameters and Query Strings

Rocket also supports **query parameters** and **URL parameters**. Here's an example of how to handle a route that accepts a query parameter:

rust

```
#[get("/greet?<name>")]
fn greet(name: Option<String>) -> String {
    match name {
        Some(name) => format!("Hello, {}!", name),
        None => "Hello, world!".to_string(),
    }
}
```

- The `?<name>` syntax tells Rocket to expect a query parameter named `name`. The `Option<String>` type means the parameter is optional.
- If the user provides a name (`/greet?name=Alice`), it greets them by name; otherwise, it returns a default greeting.

3. Returning Different Types of Responses

Rocket provides several ways to return responses, including simple strings, HTML content, JSON, and more. For example, you can return a JSON response using Rocket's `Json` type:

rust

```
use rocket::serde::{Serialize, json::Json};

#[derive(Serialize)]
struct Person {
    name: String,
    age: u32,
}

#[get("/person")]
fn person() -> Json<Person> {
    Json(Person {
        name: "Alice".to_string(),
        age: 30,
    })
}
```

- The `Json` type automatically serializes the `Person` struct into JSON format before sending the response.

Implementing Form Handling and Templates

In many web applications, you'll need to accept **form submissions** and render **HTML templates**. Rocket makes both tasks easy.

1. Handling Forms

Rocket has built-in support for form handling. To handle form data, you can use the `Form` type. Here's how you can define a route that handles a form submission:

```rust
use rocket::form::Form;

#[derive(FromForm)]
struct PersonForm {
    name: String,
    age: u32,
}

#[post("/submit_form", data = "<person>")]
fn submit_form(person: Form<PersonForm>) -> String {
    format!("Received form data: Name: {}, Age: {}",
person.name, person.age)
}
```

- `Form<PersonForm>` automatically parses the incoming form data into the `PersonForm` struct.
- The `#[derive(FromForm)]` macro generates code that allows Rocket to automatically parse the form fields.

2. Rendering Templates

To render HTML templates in Rocket, you can use the `tera` template engine, which is a powerful template engine that integrates easily with Rocket.

First, add `tera` as a dependency in your `Cargo.toml`:

toml

```toml
[dependencies]
rocket = "0.5.0-rc.2"
tera = "1.10.0"
```

Next, create a template file `templates/hello.html.tera`:

html

```html
<!DOCTYPE html>
<html>
    <head>
        <title>Hello, {{ name }}!</title>
    </head>
    <body>
        <h1>Hello, {{ name }}!</h1>
    </body>
</html>
```

In your main application, set up the `Tera` template engine:

rust

```rust
use rocket::response::content::Html;
use rocket::State;
use tera::{Tera, Context};

#[get("/greet/<name>")]
fn greet(name: String, tera: &State<Tera>) ->
Html<String> {
    let mut context = Context::new();
    context.insert("name", &name);
    let rendered = tera.render("hello.html.tera",
&context).unwrap();
    Html(rendered)
}

#[launch]
fn rocket() -> _ {
```

```
rocket::build()
    .mount("/", routes![greet])
    .manage(Tera::new("templates/**/*").unwrap())
}
```

In this example:

- **Tera::new("templates/**/*")** loads the templates from the `templates/` directory.
- The `greet` function renders the `hello.html.tera` template and inserts the `name` into the template's context.

Hands-on Project: Build a Simple CRUD Web Application with Rocket

Now that you've learned the basics of routing, handling requests, working with forms, and rendering templates, let's build a **simple CRUD (Create, Read, Update, Delete)** web application using Rocket. This application will manage a list of users, allowing users to add, view, and delete entries.

1. Set Up the Project

Create a new project:

bash

```
cargo new user_crud
cd user_crud
```

Add the following dependencies to `Cargo.toml`:

toml

```
[dependencies]
```

```
rocket = "0.5.0-rc.2"
rocket_sync_db_pools = "0.1"
serde = { version = "1.0", features = ["derive"] }
serde_json = "1.0"
```

2. Define the User Struct and Routes

In `src/main.rs`, define the `User` struct and the routes for the CRUD operations:

rust

```rust
#[macro_use] extern crate rocket;
use rocket::serde::{json::Json, Deserialize,
Serialize};

#[derive(Serialize, Deserialize, Clone)]
struct User {
    id: u32,
    name: String,
    email: String,
}

#[post("/user", data = "<user>")]
fn create_user(user: Json<User>) -> Json<User> {
    // In a real app, you'd save the user to a
database here
    Json(user.into_inner())
}

#[get("/user/<id>")]
fn get_user(id: u32) -> Option<Json<User>> {
    // Here, we mock a user for demonstration
    if id == 1 {
        Some(Json(User {
            id,
            name: String::from("Alice"),
            email: String::from("alice@example.com"),
        }))
    } else {
        None
    }
}
```

```
#[delete("/user/<id>")]
fn delete_user(id: u32) -> String {
    // In a real app, you'd delete the user from the
database
    format!("User with ID {} has been deleted.", id)
}

#[launch]
fn rocket() -> _ {
    rocket::build()
        .mount("/", routes![create_user, get_user,
delete_user])
}
```

3. Explanation

In this code:

- The `User` struct represents a user with `id`, `name`, and `email`.
- We define three routes:
    - `POST /user`: Creates a new user (in this example, we just return the user as JSON).
    - `GET /user/<id>`: Retrieves a user by their `id`.
    - `DELETE /user/<id>`: Deletes a user by their `id`.

In a real-world scenario, you would integrate a database to store and retrieve user data. For simplicity, we mock the data and logic here.

4. Testing the Application

To run the application, use the following command:

```bash
cargo run
```

You can now interact with your web app through a tool like **Postman** or **cURL**.

- **Create a User**: Send a `POST` request to `/user` with a JSON payload:

```json
{
    "id": 1,
    "name": "Alice",
    "email": "alice@example.com"
}
```

- **Get a User**: Send a `GET` request to `/user/1` to retrieve Alice's data.
- **Delete a User**: Send a `DELETE` request to `/user/1` to delete the user.

Conclusion

In this chapter, you learned how to build web applications using **Rocket**, a fast and flexible web framework for Rust. We covered everything from setting up Rocket, defining routes, handling requests and responses, to implementing form handling and templates. We also completed a hands-on project to build a **simple CRUD web application** that allows you to manage user data.

Chapter 11: Rust for Networking: Building a Web Server

Overview: Learn the Fundamentals of Networking in Rust

Networking is a crucial part of modern software development, and Rust provides powerful tools for building fast, reliable, and secure networked applications. Whether you're building a web server, a chat application, or a custom protocol, Rust's strong type system, memory safety features, and concurrency model make it an excellent choice for networking projects.

In this chapter, we'll learn how to work with networking in Rust. We will start with the basics, such as **TCP** and **UDP sockets**, and move on to more advanced concepts like **asynchronous networking** using the **Tokio** runtime. Finally, we'll build a hands-on project: a **chat server** that can handle multiple clients using Rust's asynchronous features.

By the end of this chapter, you'll have a solid understanding of how to build networked applications in Rust, from low-level socket programming to high-level asynchronous networking.

Working with TCP and UDP Sockets in Rust

Rust provides the `std::net` module, which includes types for working with both **TCP** and **UDP** sockets. Understanding how to use these sockets is key for building networked applications.

1. TCP Sockets in Rust

The **TCP** (Transmission Control Protocol) is a connection-oriented protocol. It guarantees reliable, ordered delivery of data between applications running on different machines. With TCP, you can create a server that listens for incoming connections, and a client that connects to the server to exchange data.

Let's start by building a simple **TCP server** and **client** in Rust.

TCP Server:

Here's how to create a TCP server that listens for incoming connections:

```rust
use std::net::{TcpListener, TcpStream};
use std::io::{Read, Write};
use std::thread;

fn handle_client(mut stream: TcpStream) {
    let mut buffer = [0; 512];
    match stream.read(&mut buffer) {
        Ok(bytes_read) => {
            if bytes_read == 0 {
                return;
            }

stream.write(&buffer[0..bytes_read]).unwrap();
        }
        Err(e) => eprintln!("Error reading from
stream: {}", e),
    }
}

fn main() {
```

```
    let listener =
TcpListener::bind("127.0.0.1:7878").expect("Could not
bind to address");

    println!("Server is running on 127.0.0.1:7878");

    for stream in listener.incoming() {
        match stream {
            Ok(stream) => {
                thread::spawn(move || {
                    handle_client(stream);
                });
            }
            Err(e) => eprintln!("Failed to accept
connection: {}", e),
        }
    }
}
```

Explanation:

- The `TcpListener::bind` method binds the server to a specific IP address and port. In this case, the server listens on `127.0.0.1:7878` (localhost).
- The `listener.incoming()` method returns an iterator over incoming `TcpStream`s.
- For each incoming connection, we spawn a new thread to handle the client. This way, the server can handle multiple clients simultaneously.
- The `handle_client` function reads data from the stream and echoes it back to the client.

TCP Client:

Now, let's create a simple **TCP client** that connects to the server:

```rust
```

```
use std::net::TcpStream;
use std::io::{Read, Write};

fn main() {
    let mut stream =
TcpStream::connect("127.0.0.1:7878").expect("Could
not connect to server");

    let msg = b"Hello, server!";
    stream.write(msg).expect("Failed to send
message");

    let mut buffer = [0; 512];
    let bytes_read = stream.read(&mut
buffer).expect("Failed to read response");

    println!("Server replied: {}",
String::from_utf8_lossy(&buffer[0..bytes_read]));
}
```

Explanation:

- The client connects to the server using `TcpStream::connect`.
- It sends a message to the server using `stream.write`.
- The client then waits for the server's response, reads the data into a buffer, and prints it.

You can run the server and client in separate terminals to test the communication between them. The server will echo the message sent by the client.

2. UDP Sockets in Rust

Unlike TCP, **UDP** (User Datagram Protocol) is a connectionless protocol. It doesn't guarantee the order or reliability of data delivery, but it is faster because it doesn't require a connection to be established or maintain state. UDP is useful for applications that prioritize speed over reliability, such as real-time streaming or multiplayer games.

Let's now build a simple **UDP server** and **client**.

UDP Server:

```rust
use std::net::UdpSocket;

fn main() {
    let socket =
UdpSocket::bind("127.0.0.1:7878").expect("Could not
bind to address");

    let mut buf = [0; 512];
    loop {
        let (amt, src) = socket.recv_from(&mut
buf).expect("Failed to receive data");
        println!("Received data: {}",
String::from_utf8_lossy(&buf[0..amt]));

        socket.send_to(&buf[0..amt],
&src).expect("Failed to send response");
    }
}
```

Explanation:

- The `UdpSocket::bind` method binds the server to the given address and port.
- The `recv_from` method waits for incoming data and returns the number of bytes read and the source address of the sender.
- The server then echoes the received data back to the sender using `send_to`.

UDP Client:

```rust
use std::net::UdpSocket;

fn main() {
    let socket =
UdpSocket::bind("127.0.0.1:0").expect("Could not bind
to address");

    let server_addr = "127.0.0.1:7878";
    let msg = b"Hello, server!";
    socket.send_to(msg, server_addr).expect("Failed
to send message");

    let mut buf = [0; 512];
    let (amt, _src) = socket.recv_from(&mut
buf).expect("Failed to receive data");

    println!("Server replied: {}",
String::from_utf8_lossy(&buf[0..amt]));
}
```

Explanation:

- The `UdpSocket::bind` method binds the client to a random available port (`127.0.0.1:0`).
- The client sends a message to the server using `send_to` and then waits for a response using `recv_from`.

Building a Simple HTTP Server

Now that we understand basic networking with TCP and UDP, let's take a look at how to build a simple **HTTP server** in Rust. HTTP (Hypertext Transfer Protocol) is the foundation of data communication on the web. While Rust has lower-level libraries for working with TCP and UDP, building an HTTP server from scratch can be complex. Fortunately, libraries like **Hyper** and **Rocket** make this process easier.

Here, we will build a simple HTTP server from scratch using **Hyper**, a low-level HTTP library for Rust.

1. Setting Up Hyper

First, add the `hyper` crate to your `Cargo.toml` file:

```toml
[dependencies]
hyper = "0.14"
tokio = { version = "1", features = ["full"] }
```

Now, let's create a basic HTTP server that listens on port `8080` and responds with a simple message.

```rust
use hyper::{Body, Request, Response, Server};
use hyper::service::{make_service_fn, service_fn};

async fn handle_request(req: Request<Body>) ->
Result<Response<Body>, hyper::Error> {
    Ok(Response::new(Body::from("Hello, World!")))
}

#[tokio::main]
async fn main() {
    let make_svc = make_service_fn(|_conn| async {
        Ok::<_,
hyper::Error>(service_fn(handle_request))
    });

    let addr = ([127, 0, 0, 1], 8080).into();
    let server = Server::bind(&addr).serve(make_svc);

    println!("Listening on http://{}", addr);
    if let Err(e) = server.await {
        eprintln!("Server error: {}", e);
    }
}
```

Explanation:

- We use **Hyper** to set up an HTTP server. The server listens on `127.0.0.1:8080`.
- The `handle_request` function returns a simple "Hello, World!" message for any incoming request.
- The server is asynchronous, running on **Tokio**, Rust's asynchronous runtime, which allows it to handle multiple requests concurrently.

To run this server, simply execute:

```bash
cargo run
```

You can test it by navigating to `http://127.0.0.1:8080` in your browser or using **cURL**:

```bash
curl http://127.0.0.1:8080
```

This should return the message `Hello, World!`.

Asynchronous Networking with Tokio

In the examples above, we built simple servers using synchronous blocking calls. However, in real-world applications, especially those dealing with many simultaneous connections, asynchronous programming is essential for scalability and performance.

Rust's async model, powered by **Tokio**, allows you to handle multiple I/O-bound operations concurrently without blocking threads. This makes it possible to efficiently handle many requests in parallel, without creating new threads for each connection.

1. Asynchronous Networking with Tokio

To demonstrate asynchronous networking, let's rewrite the TCP server example to use Tokio. This will allow the server to handle multiple client connections concurrently without blocking.

Here's a simple **asynchronous TCP server** using Tokio:

```rust
use tokio::net::TcpListener;
use tokio::io::{AsyncReadExt, AsyncWriteExt};

async fn handle_client(mut socket:
tokio::net::TcpStream) {
    let mut buffer = vec![0; 1024];
    loop {
        let n = match socket.read(&mut buffer).await
{
            Ok(n) if n == 0 => return,
            Ok(n) => n,
            Err(e) => {
                eprintln!("Failed to read from
socket: {}", e);
                return;
            }
        };
        if
socket.write_all(&buffer[0..n]).await.is_err() {
            eprintln!("Failed to write to socket");
            return;
        }
    }
}
```

```
#[tokio::main]
async fn main() {
    let listener =
TcpListener::bind("127.0.0.1:7878")
        .await
        .expect("Failed to bind address");

    println!("Server running on 127.0.0.1:7878");

    loop {
        let (socket, _) =
listener.accept().await.expect("Failed to accept
connection");
        tokio::spawn(async move {
            handle_client(socket).await;
        });
    }
}
```

Explanation:

- We use **Tokio's** `TcpListener` to asynchronously listen for incoming connections.
- Each connection is handled by the `handle_client` function, which reads from the socket and then writes the same data back to the client (echoing).
- **Tokio's** `spawn` allows us to handle each client connection concurrently in a non-blocking manner.

This example shows how you can handle multiple TCP connections without blocking the main thread, which is essential for building high-performance networked applications.

Hands-on Project: Create a Basic Chat Server That Handles Multiple Clients Using Rust's Async Features

Let's take what we've learned and build a **basic chat server** that allows multiple clients to connect and send messages to each other. This chat server will handle multiple clients asynchronously using **Tokio**.

1. Set Up the Project

Create a new project:

bash

```bash
cargo new chat_server
cd chat_server
```

Add the dependencies to `Cargo.toml`:

toml

```toml
[dependencies]
tokio = { version = "1", features = ["full"] }
futures = "0.3"
```

2. Build the Chat Server

In `src/main.rs`, write the following code:

rust

```rust
use tokio::net::{TcpListener, TcpStream};
use tokio::sync::{broadcast, Mutex};
use tokio::io::{AsyncReadExt, AsyncWriteExt};
use std::sync::Arc;

async fn handle_client(mut socket: TcpStream, tx:
Arc<Mutex<broadcast::Sender<String>>>) {
    let (mut reader, mut writer) = socket.split();
    let mut rx = tx.lock().await.subscribe();
```

```
    let mut buffer = vec![0; 1024];

    loop {
        tokio::select! {
            result = reader.read(&mut buffer) => {
                match result {
                    Ok(0) => break, // Connection
closed
                    Ok(n) => {
                        let msg =
String::from_utf8_lossy(&buffer[0..n]).to_string();

tx.lock().await.send(msg).unwrap(); // Broadcast the
message
                    },
                    Err(_) => break, // Error reading
from socket
                }
            }
            result = rx.recv() => {
                match result {
                    Ok(msg) =>
writer.write_all(msg.as_bytes()).await.unwrap(), //
Send message to client
                    Err(_) => break, // Error
receiving message
                }
            }
        }
    }
}

#[tokio::main]
async fn main() {
    let listener =
TcpListener::bind("127.0.0.1:8080").await.unwrap();
    let (tx, _rx) =
broadcast::channel::<String>(100);
    let tx = Arc::new(Mutex::new(tx));

    println!("Chat server running on
127.0.0.1:8080");
```

```
    loop {
        let (socket, _) =
listener.accept().await.unwrap();
        let tx = tx.clone();
        tokio::spawn(async move {
            handle_client(socket, tx).await;
        });
    }
}
```

Explanation:

- We use **Tokio's** `TcpListener` to accept incoming connections asynchronously.
- Each client's connection is handled by the `handle_client` function, which reads messages from the client and broadcasts them to all other clients using a **broadcast channel**.
- The `broadcast::Sender` allows us to send messages to all connected clients.
- Each client's messages are read asynchronously, and the server sends the received message to all other clients.

3. Testing the Chat Server

To test the chat server, you can use multiple terminal windows and connect to the server using `telnet` or any TCP client. In one terminal, run:

```bash

cargo run
```

In another terminal, connect to the chat server:

```bash
```

```
telnet 127.0.0.1 8080
```

Repeat the process in multiple terminals to simulate multiple clients. Messages sent by one client will be broadcast to all other connected clients.

Conclusion

In this chapter, we've explored how to build networked applications using Rust. We started by learning about **TCP and UDP sockets**, which are the foundation of networking in Rust. We then built a **simple HTTP server** using **Hyper**, and explored **asynchronous networking** with **Tokio**.

Finally, we applied these concepts to build a **chat server** that can handle multiple clients asynchronously. Using Rust's async features and **Tokio**, we were able to handle many clients concurrently without blocking, making the server fast and efficient.

Chapter 12: Rust for Embedded Systems Programming

Overview: Introduction to Rust in the World of Embedded Systems

Embedded systems are specialized computing systems that interact with hardware and perform dedicated functions. These systems are found in everyday devices such as cars, medical devices, IoT gadgets, and household appliances. Unlike general-purpose computers, embedded systems often have stringent requirements, including low power consumption, real-time performance, and high reliability.

Rust, with its focus on performance, safety, and control over system resources, has gained significant attention in the embedded systems programming world. Its memory safety guarantees—without a garbage collector—make it particularly suited for environments where resources are limited and reliability is critical. Rust's ownership model ensures that developers can write safe, efficient code for embedded systems while avoiding the pitfalls of common low-level errors like buffer overflows, null pointer dereferencing, and race conditions.

In this chapter, we'll introduce you to the world of embedded systems programming with Rust. We will explore why Rust is a perfect choice for embedded development, how to set up a Rust environment for embedded systems, and how to interact with hardware. Finally, we'll build a simple project—a **LED blinking program**—to demonstrate how Rust can be used in real-world embedded applications.

Why Rust is Perfect for Low-Level Embedded Systems

Embedded systems programming requires direct interaction with hardware. This often involves working with constrained resources, such as limited memory and processing power. Additionally, embedded systems must meet strict reliability requirements because they are typically embedded into critical applications like automotive systems, medical devices, and industrial controls.

Rust's combination of performance and safety features makes it uniquely suited for these types of applications. Here's why:

1. Memory Safety Without Garbage Collection

Unlike many traditional high-level languages that rely on garbage collection to manage memory, Rust provides **manual memory management** through its **ownership system**. This ensures that memory is freed when it is no longer needed, but without the runtime overhead of garbage collection. This is crucial in embedded systems, where every byte counts and predictable behavior is required.

Rust ensures that memory access is safe through its **ownership model**. The compiler tracks ownership and ensures that there are no dangling pointers, double frees, or data races, even in multi-threaded applications. This is particularly beneficial when developing low-level software where developers need full control over hardware resources.

2. Concurrency and Parallelism

Rust offers powerful concurrency features through **async/await** syntax and **message passing**. Rust's concurrency model ensures that data races are prevented, even in highly concurrent applications, making it ideal for building multi-threaded applications on embedded platforms.

This is essential in embedded systems, where multiple processes (e.g., sensors, actuators) often need to run concurrently and interact with each other in real-time.

3. Minimal Runtime and No Standard Library for Embedded Systems

In embedded systems, having a minimal runtime is critical. Rust's flexibility allows it to be used without the standard library (`#![no_std]`), which is often required when working with microcontrollers and other resource-constrained devices. By removing the standard library, you can eliminate unnecessary overhead and tailor the runtime to the specific requirements of the embedded system.

Rust's ability to compile to bare-metal code—without a large runtime or operating system—makes it perfect for embedded systems where low-level access to hardware is necessary.

4. Cross-Platform Compatibility

Rust has excellent support for cross-compiling, which is particularly useful in embedded development. With Rust, you can easily cross-compile your code for different architectures, such as ARM, RISC-V, and x86. This feature allows you to target a wide range of embedded devices without worrying about compatibility issues.

Setting Up a Rust Environment for Embedded Systems

Setting up a Rust environment for embedded systems is slightly different from traditional Rust development. The typical Rust development setup involves installing `rustup` (the Rust toolchain installer) and using the default target (e.g., x86_64). However, for embedded systems, we need to set up a **cross-compilation toolchain** that allows Rust to target platforms like ARM microcontrollers, Raspberry Pi, or other bare-metal systems.

1. Installing Rust

First, install the standard Rust toolchain if you haven't already:

bash

```
curl --proto '=https' --tlsv1.2 -sSf
https://sh.rustup.rs | sh
```

After installation, you can verify your installation by running:

bash

```
rustc --version
```

2. Installing `cargo` for Cross Compilation

Rust uses the **cargo** tool to manage projects, dependencies, and builds. For embedded systems, you'll need to install additional tools to cross-compile to the target architecture.

The most common embedded targets include ARM-based devices and microcontrollers, so we'll set up the environment to compile for these targets.

To add a target for ARM-based systems, run:

```bash
rustup target add thumbv7em-none-eabihf
```

This installs the target for ARM Cortex-M devices.

3. Setting Up a Cross-Compilation Toolchain

Embedded systems often require additional tools, such as a cross-compiler and linker. For example, when working with ARM-based devices, you may need to install **arm-none-eabi** tools.

To install the `arm-none-eabi` toolchain, you can use the following command on Ubuntu:

```bash
sudo apt-get install gcc-arm-none-eabi
```

This installs the necessary tools to cross-compile for ARM microcontrollers.

4. Setting Up a `Cargo.toml` File for Embedded Systems

Once the toolchain is set up, you'll need to configure your project for **bare-metal** or **no_std** programming. This is done by adding the `#![no_std]` attribute in your `lib.rs` or `main.rs` file, which disables Rust's standard library and reduces the size of your program.

For example, in `src/main.rs`:

```rust
rust

#![no_std]
#![no_main]

use panic_halt as _; // Panic handler for embedded
systems

#[entry]
fn main() -> ! {
    loop {
        // Embedded application code here
    }
}
```

In your `Cargo.toml` file, you would specify the appropriate dependencies, which could include crate libraries that support embedded systems, such as `cortex-m`, `cortex-m-rt`, and `rtt-target`.

Accessing Hardware and Working with Memory Mapped I/O

One of the most important aspects of embedded programming is interacting with the hardware. Rust provides several crates that help you interface with **memory-mapped I/O** (MMIO), a method for controlling hardware registers directly.

1. Working with Memory Mapped Registers

In embedded systems, hardware components (e.g., GPIO, timers, UART) are typically controlled through registers, which are accessed using memory addresses. Rust allows you to safely interact with these registers by using **volatile** reads and writes, ensuring that the compiler doesn't optimize out the accesses.

Here's a simple example of how you can access a memory-mapped register for a GPIO pin:

rust

```
use core::ptr;

const GPIO_BASE: u32 = 0x5000_0000; // Base address
for GPIO registers

// Example of a register that controls the direction
of a GPIO pin
const GPIO_DIR: *mut u32 = (GPIO_BASE + 0x04) as *mut
u32;

fn set_gpio_direction() {
    unsafe {
        ptr::write_volatile(GPIO_DIR, 0x1); // Set
GPIO pin as output
    }
}
```

In this code:

- GPIO_BASE is the base address of the GPIO registers.
- We use unsafe because interacting with memory-mapped I/O is inherently unsafe in Rust.
- ptr::write_volatile writes to the GPIO direction register without optimizations, ensuring that the hardware is properly updated.

2. Handling Peripherals with Crates

Many embedded systems, like ARM Cortex-M microcontrollers, come with dedicated crates that abstract hardware access.

For example, the `cortex-m` crate provides low-level access to the Cortex-M processor, and `cortex-m-rt` provides runtime support for bare-metal applications.

To use these crates, you can add them to your `Cargo.toml` file:

toml

```
[dependencies]
cortex-m = "0.7"
cortex-m-rt = "0.6"
```

Now, you can use the APIs provided by these crates to interact with peripherals like timers, interrupts, and GPIO.

Hands-on Project: Build a Basic LED Blinking Program for an Embedded System Using Rust

Now that we've covered the fundamentals, it's time to dive into a real-world example: building a simple **LED blinking program** for an embedded system. This project will demonstrate how to write Rust code that directly controls hardware.

1. Setting Up the Project

Let's create a new project for our embedded system:

bash

```
cargo new led_blink
cd led_blink
```

In this case, we'll assume that you're targeting an ARM Cortex-M microcontroller, and we'll use the **STM32** family of microcontrollers as an example. First, add the following dependencies to your `Cargo.toml`:

```toml
[dependencies]
cortex-m = "0.7"
cortex-m-rt = "0.6"
stm32f4 = "0.9.0"
panic-halt = "0.2.0"
```

These dependencies include:

- **`cortex-m`**: Provides low-level access to the Cortex-M processor.
- **`cortex-m-rt`**: Provides runtime support for bare-metal applications.
- **`stm32f4`**: A crate that provides abstractions for the STM32F4 microcontroller family.
- **`panic-halt`**: A simple panic handler for embedded systems that halts the system on panic.

2. Writing the LED Blinking Code

In `src/main.rs`, write the following code:

```rust
#![no_std]
#![no_main]

use panic_halt as _;
use stm32f4::stm32f407;
use cortex_m::asm::delay;
use cortex_m_rt::entry;

#[entry]
fn main() -> ! {
```

```
    let peripherals =
stm32f407::Peripherals::take().unwrap();
    let gpioa = &peripherals.GPIOA;

    // Set PA5 (pin 5 on GPIOA) as output
    gpioa.moder.modify(|_, w| w.moder5().output());

    loop {
        gpioa.bsrr.write(|w| w.bs5().set_bit()); //
Set PA5 high
        delay(8_000_000); // Delay for a short time

        gpioa.bsrr.write(|w| w.br5().set_bit()); //
Set PA5 low
        delay(8_000_000); // Delay for a short time
    }
}
```

Explanation:

- **`stm32f407::Peripherals::take()`**: Retrieves the
  peripherals for the STM32F4 microcontroller.
- **GPIOA**: Refers to the General Purpose Input/Output
  (GPIO) port A.
- **`gpioa.moder.modify`**: Configures pin PA5 (which is
  connected to an onboard LED) as an output pin.
- **`gpioa.bsrr.write`**: Writes a bit to the GPIO output data
  register, controlling the state of the LED.
- **`cortex_m::asm::delay`**: Introduces a delay to make the
  LED blink at a visible rate.

3. Compiling and Flashing the Program

To compile this program, you'll need to use the `thumbv7em-none-eabihf` target for ARM Cortex-M microcontrollers:

bash

```
cargo build --target thumbv7em-none-eabihf
```

Next, you can use tools like **OpenOCD** or **ST-Link** to flash the program onto the microcontroller.

Conclusion

In this chapter, we learned how Rust can be used for **embedded systems programming**, focusing on the unique features that make Rust ideal for low-level embedded development. We explored how to set up a Rust environment for embedded systems, how to access hardware using **memory-mapped I/O**, and how to write safe, high-performance code for constrained devices.

We also built a simple **LED blinking program** for an embedded system, demonstrating how to interact directly with hardware using Rust. This hands-on project highlighted how Rust's memory safety features and control over system resources can be leveraged to build reliable embedded applications.

Rust's growing support for embedded systems, combined with its performance, safety, and concurrency features, makes it an excellent choice for a wide range of embedded applications.

Chapter 13: Advanced Rust Features: Traits, Generics, and Macros

Overview: Go Deeper into Rust's Advanced Features that Provide Flexibility and Power

Rust is a language that allows developers to write **high-performance**, **reliable**, and **safe** code, but what truly sets Rust apart is its ability to provide advanced features that enhance **flexibility** and **expressiveness**. In this chapter, we will explore three of Rust's most powerful and flexible features: **Traits**, **Generics**, and **Macros**. These features give you the ability to write **generic**, **polymorphic**, and **meta-programming** code that is both **safe** and **efficient**.

Each of these features can be seen as a tool that enables a different form of abstraction, making your Rust code not only more reusable but also more **expressive** and **maintainable**.

By the end of this chapter, you'll have a deeper understanding of how to leverage these advanced features to write **cleaner**, **more reusable**, and **more flexible** Rust code. We'll also apply these features in a **hands-on project** where we will create a **custom collection type** using **generics**, implement several methods using **traits**, and explore how **macros** can simplify the creation of complex functionality.

Understanding Traits and How They Enable Polymorphism

Traits are one of the cornerstones of Rust's type system, enabling polymorphism without the need for runtime dynamic dispatch. In simple terms, a trait defines a set of methods that a type must implement. This allows different types to share common behavior, and the trait system provides **polymorphism**—the ability for different types to be treated as the same type through a common interface.

1. What is a Trait?

A **trait** in Rust is similar to an interface in other languages. It defines functionality that types must implement but does not provide the implementation itself. Traits enable you to write **generic** code that works with any type that implements a particular trait.

Here's an example of a simple trait:

rust

```
// Define a trait
trait Speak {
    fn speak(&self);
}

// Implement the trait for a specific type
struct Dog;
impl Speak for Dog {
    fn speak(&self) {
        println!("Woof!");
    }
}

struct Cat;
impl Speak for Cat {
    fn speak(&self) {
```

```
        println!("Meow!");
    }
}

fn main() {
    let dog = Dog;
    let cat = Cat;

    dog.speak();   // Outputs: Woof!
    cat.speak();   // Outputs: Meow!
}
```

In this example:

- The `Speak` trait defines a method `speak`, but it doesn't provide an implementation.
- Both `Dog` and `Cat` implement the `Speak` trait, providing their own implementation of the `speak` method.
- The `main` function demonstrates polymorphism, where both `dog` and `cat` are treated as objects that can `speak`, even though they are different types.

2. Trait Bounds and Polymorphism

Rust allows you to write **generic** functions and structs that can work with any type that implements a particular trait. This is achieved through **trait bounds**. Trait bounds allow you to specify that a generic type must implement a specific trait before you can call methods defined in that trait.

Here's an example of using trait bounds with a generic function:

```
rust

fn greet<T: Speak>(item: T) {
    item.speak();
}
```

```
fn main() {
    let dog = Dog;
    let cat = Cat;

    greet(dog);   // Outputs: Woof!
    greet(cat);   // Outputs: Meow!
}
```

In this example:

- The function `greet` accepts a parameter of any type `T` that implements the `Speak` trait.
- The `T: Speak` syntax is a trait bound, meaning `greet` can only be called with types that implement the `Speak` trait.

Trait bounds can also be used in structs and other types, enabling **polymorphism** and **type safety** at compile time.

3. Default Method Implementations in Traits

One of the powerful features of traits in Rust is that you can provide **default method implementations**. This allows types that implement the trait to inherit default behavior unless they explicitly override it.

rust

```
trait Speak {
    fn speak(&self) {
        println!("Some generic sound");
    }
}

struct Dog;

impl Speak for Dog {
    fn speak(&self) {
```

```
        println!("Woof!");
    }
}

fn main() {
    let dog = Dog;
    dog.speak();  // Outputs: Woof!
}
```

In this example:

- The `Speak` trait has a default implementation of `speak`, which outputs `"Some generic sound"`.
- `Dog` implements `speak`, so the default implementation is overridden.
- This allows you to provide common behavior across many types while still allowing for custom behavior when necessary.

Working with Generics for Type Safety and Reusability

Generics are one of the most powerful features of Rust, enabling **type safety** and **reusability** in your code. Generics allow you to write **flexible** functions, structs, and enums that can work with any type, all while maintaining type safety and performance.

1. What are Generics?

Generics allow you to write functions, structs, and enums that can work with different types. For example, you can write a function that works with any type of number, such as `i32` or `f64`, without duplicating code for each specific type.

Here's a simple example of a generic function:

```rust
fn print_item<T>(item: T) {
    println!("{:?}", item);
}

fn main() {
    print_item(42);  // Prints: 42
    print_item("Hello, world!");  // Prints: Hello,
world!
}
```

In this example:

- The function `print_item` is generic over type `T`.
- It works with any type `T`, and the Rust compiler will generate the appropriate code for each type used with the function.

2. Generic Structs and Enums

You can also define **generic structs** and **generic enums**. This allows you to create data structures that can store any type of data.

```rust
struct Pair<T, U> {
    first: T,
    second: U,
}

impl<T, U> Pair<T, U> {
    fn new(first: T, second: U) -> Self {
        Pair { first, second }
    }

    fn display(&self) {
        println!("First: {:?}, Second: {:?}",
self.first, self.second);
```

```
    }
}

fn main() {
    let pair = Pair::new(1, "one");
    pair.display();   // Outputs: First: 1, Second:
"one"
}
```

In this example:

- `Pair` is a struct that holds two values, each of a different type (`T` and `U`).
- The `new` method creates a new `Pair`, and the `display` method prints the values.

3. Generic Methods with Constraints

In Rust, you can also add constraints to generics using **trait bounds**. This ensures that the type used with a generic parameter must implement a specific trait.

rust

```
fn print_len<T: std::fmt::Debug>(item: T) {
    println!("{:?}", item);
}

fn main() {
    print_len("Hello, Rust!");   // Prints: "Hello,
Rust!"
    print_len(42);   // Prints: 42
}
```

In this example:

- The `print_len` function is constrained by `T: std::fmt::Debug`, which means that `T` must implement the `Debug` trait.

Using Macros to Reduce Repetitive Code

Macros in Rust provide a powerful way to reduce repetitive code and generate complex functionality at compile time. Rust macros are similar to those in other languages, but they are more powerful and flexible due to their integration with the Rust compiler.

1. What Are Macros?

A macro is a way to write code that writes other code. Instead of manually writing repetitive code, you can define a macro that generates the code for you. Rust macros can operate on any part of the code, including functions, structs, enums, and even syntax.

Here's a simple example of a macro that takes two numbers and adds them together:

```rust
rust

macro_rules! add {
    ($a:expr, $b:expr) => {
        $a + $b
    };
}

fn main() {
    let result = add!(5, 10);
    println!("The result is: {}", result);   //
Outputs: The result is: 15
}
```

In this example:

- The `add!` macro takes two expressions (`$a` and `$b`) and returns their sum.
- The macro is expanded at compile time into the code that performs the addition.

2. Defining Macros with More Complex Logic

Macros in Rust can be more complex than simple value substitution. They can accept patterns and generate code based on those patterns. Here's an example of a macro that creates multiple functions:

rust

```
macro_rules! create_functions {
    ($($name:ident),*) => {
        $(
            fn $name() {
                println!("Function {} was called!",
stringify!($name));
            }
        )*
    };
}

create_functions!(foo, bar, baz);

fn main() {
    foo();   // Outputs: Function foo was called!
    bar();   // Outputs: Function bar was called!
    baz();   // Outputs: Function baz was called!
}
```

In this example:

- The `create_functions!` macro takes a list of function names and generates functions with those names.
- `stringify!($name)` converts the function name to a string for display in the `println!` statement.

3. Macros for Repeated Code Patterns

Rust macros are ideal for reducing boilerplate code. For instance, you can define a macro that handles common patterns for implementing methods on structs:

```rust
macro_rules! create_method {
    ($name:ident, $ty:ty) => {
        fn $name(&self) -> $ty {
            // Return a default value of the
specified type
            Default::default()
        }
    };
}

struct MyStruct;

impl MyStruct {
    create_method!(get_value, i32);
}

fn main() {
    let my_struct = MyStruct;
    println!("{}", my_struct.get_value());   //
Outputs: 0
}
```

This example:

- Defines a macro `create_method!` that generates a method with a specified name and return type.
- The `get_value` method is created on `MyStruct`, returning a default value for `i32` (which is `0`).

Hands-on Project: Create a Custom Collection Type with Generics, and Implement Several Methods Using Traits

Now that we've covered the basics of **traits, generics**, and **macros**, let's create a **custom collection type** using **generics** and **traits**. We will build a simple **stack** data structure that can store any type and implement methods like `push`, `pop`, and `peek`.

1. Set Up the Project

Create a new project:

bash

```
cargo new custom_collection
cd custom_collection
```

2. Define the Stack Struct

In `src/main.rs`, define a `Stack` struct with a generic type:

rust

```
#[derive(Debug)]
struct Stack<T> {
    items: Vec<T>,
}

impl<T> Stack<T> {
    fn new() -> Self {
        Stack { items: Vec::new() }
    }

    fn push(&mut self, item: T) {
        self.items.push(item);
    }

    fn pop(&mut self) -> Option<T> {
        self.items.pop()
```

```
    }

    fn peek(&self) -> Option<&T> {
        self.items.last()
    }
}

fn main() {
    let mut stack = Stack::new();
    stack.push(1);
    stack.push(2);
    stack.push(3);

    println!("{:?}", stack.peek());   // Some(3)
    println!("{:?}", stack.pop());    // Some(3)
    println!("{:?}", stack.peek());   // Some(2)
}
```

3. Explanation

- `Stack<T>` is a generic struct that stores a vector of items.
- The `push` method adds an item to the stack, `pop` removes the top item, and `peek` retrieves the top item without removing it.
- We use **generics** (T) to allow the stack to store any type.

4. Testing the Collection

The example above demonstrates how to use the stack to store integers. You can modify it to store other types (e.g., strings, floats) and test the methods by adding and removing items.

Conclusion

In this chapter, we delved into three of Rust's most advanced and powerful features: **traits**, **generics**, and **macros**. These features empower you to write **flexible, type-safe**, and **reusable** code. We learned how traits enable polymorphism and how generics provide the ability to write code that works with multiple types while maintaining type safety. We also saw how macros can reduce boilerplate and simplify complex patterns in your code.

Through our hands-on project, we created a **custom collection type** using generics and implemented methods using traits. This project demonstrated how to apply these advanced features to solve real-world problems and write efficient, reusable code.

Chapter 14: Testing and Benchmarking in Rust

Overview: Learn the Best Practices for Writing Tests and Benchmarks in Rust

Writing tests and benchmarks is a crucial part of any software development process. In Rust, testing and performance benchmarking are given top priority to ensure **reliability**, **correctness**, and **optimal performance**. Whether you're working on a simple utility or a large-scale system, testing ensures that your code behaves as expected, and benchmarking guarantees that your application runs efficiently.

In this chapter, we'll explore Rust's built-in testing framework, show you how to write different types of tests, and dive into performance benchmarking with **Criterion**, a powerful benchmarking library for Rust. By the end of this chapter, you'll know how to ensure the correctness and efficiency of your code by applying Rust's best practices for testing and benchmarking.

Rust's Built-in Testing Framework

Rust comes with a built-in testing framework that is easy to use and integrated into the language. The framework supports unit tests, integration tests, and even property-based testing. The testing system is part of the Rust toolchain, which means you don't need any additional libraries or dependencies to get started with testing.

1. Unit Testing in Rust

A **unit test** focuses on testing small units of functionality in isolation. In Rust, unit tests are written within the same file as the code being tested and are located in a `#[cfg(test)]` module. This module is only included when testing is enabled, ensuring that your tests do not end up in production code.

Here's a simple example of a unit test:

rust

```
fn add_two_numbers(a: i32, b: i32) -> i32 {
    a + b
}

#[cfg(test)]
mod tests {
    use super::*;   // Import all the items from the
outer scope

    #[test]
    fn test_add_two_numbers() {
        let result = add_two_numbers(2, 3);
        assert_eq!(result, 5);
    }
}
```

Explanation:

- `#[cfg(test)]`: This attribute marks the module for testing, so it will only be included during the test phase.
- `#[test]`: Marks a function as a test function.
- `assert_eq!(result, 5)`: This macro checks if `result` is equal to `5`. If it is, the test passes; if not, the test fails.

2. Integration Testing in Rust

While unit tests test individual functions, **integration tests** focus on testing how different parts of your code work together. These tests are typically placed in a separate directory called `tests`.

Here's an example of an integration test:

```rust
// File: tests/integration_test.rs

use my_project::add_two_numbers;

#[test]
fn test_integration_addition() {
    let result = add_two_numbers(5, 7);
    assert_eq!(result, 12);
}
```

Explanation:

- This test resides in the `tests` directory, separate from the main source code.
- It calls the `add_two_numbers` function from the main project and ensures that it works as expected in an integrated environment.

3. Testing with External Crates

You may want to test your code with external crates like `serde` or `tokio`. Rust's testing framework works seamlessly with third-party crates, and you can include them in your tests just like regular Rust code.

Here's an example of a test that involves an external crate:

```rust
use serde::{Serialize, Deserialize};
use serde_json;

#[derive(Serialize, Deserialize, PartialEq, Debug)]
struct Person {
    name: String,
    age: u32,
}

#[cfg(test)]
mod tests {
    use super::*;

    #[test]
    fn test_serialization() {
        let person = Person {
            name: String::from("Alice"),
            age: 30,
        };

        let json =
serde_json::to_string(&person).unwrap();
        let expected_json =
r#"{"name":"Alice","age":30}"#;
        assert_eq!(json, expected_json);
    }
}
```

Explanation:

- This test checks if the `Person` struct can be serialized to JSON using the `serde` crate.
- It uses `serde_json::to_string` to convert the `Person` struct into a JSON string and then compares the output with the expected JSON.

4. Property-Based Testing

In addition to writing tests for specific cases, Rust allows you to do **property-based testing**, where you test the properties of your code over a large set of input values. The `proptest` crate is widely used for property-based testing in Rust.

Here's an example using `proptest`:

```toml
[dependencies]
proptest = "1.0"
```

```rust
use proptest::prelude::*;

proptest! {
    #[test]
    fn test_addition(a: i32, b: i32) {
        prop_assert_eq!(a + b, b + a);   // 
Commutativity of addition
    }
}
```

Explanation:

- `proptest!` is a macro that generates test cases for the `test_addition` function.
- `prop_assert_eq!` is used to assert that the addition operation is **commutative** (i.e., `a + b` should equal `b + a`).

Benchmarking Code Performance with Criterion

While writing correct code is important, ensuring that your code runs efficiently is equally crucial. **Benchmarking** helps you measure the performance of your code and identify bottlenecks. In Rust, the **Criterion** crate is a powerful and flexible benchmarking library that provides easy-to-use tools for performance testing.

1. Setting Up Criterion

To get started with Criterion, add it to your `Cargo.toml` file:

toml

```
[dependencies]
criterion = "0.3"
```

Then, create a new file `benches/benchmark.rs` where you'll write your benchmark tests.

rust

```
use criterion::{black_box, criterion_group,
criterion_main, Criterion};

fn bench_addition(c: &mut Criterion) {
    c.bench_function("add two numbers", |b| {
        b.iter(|| black_box(2 + 3)) // Benchmark the
addition operation
    });
}

criterion_group!(benches, bench_addition);
criterion_main!(benches);
```

Explanation:

- `criterion_group!` defines a group of benchmarks, and `criterion_main!` sets up the benchmark runner.
- `black_box` ensures that the compiler doesn't optimize away the addition operation during benchmarking.
- `b.iter()` repeatedly runs the benchmarked code, measuring its performance.

2. Running Benchmarks

To run your benchmarks, use the following command:

```bash
cargo bench
```

This will run all the benchmarks defined in the `benches` directory and provide detailed statistics about execution time, helping you spot performance regressions or bottlenecks.

3. Benchmark Results

After running the benchmarks, Criterion will provide detailed output, including:

- The **mean** execution time.
- The **standard deviation** (variability of performance).
- A **comparison** of results across different benchmarks.

Hands-on Project: Create a Simple Application and Write Tests to Ensure Correctness

Now that we understand how to write tests and benchmarks in Rust, let's apply this knowledge by creating a simple application and ensuring its correctness with tests and performance measurements.

We'll create a basic **calculator application** that supports addition, subtraction, multiplication, and division. We'll then write unit tests to verify that the application functions correctly and use Criterion to benchmark the performance of the arithmetic operations.

1. Create the Calculator Application

Let's start by creating the calculator logic in `src/main.rs`:

```rust
rust

pub fn add(a: i32, b: i32) -> i32 {
    a + b
}

pub fn subtract(a: i32, b: i32) -> i32 {
    a - b
}

pub fn multiply(a: i32, b: i32) -> i32 {
    a * b
}

pub fn divide(a: i32, b: i32) -> Result<i32, String>
{
    if b == 0 {
        Err(String::from("Division by zero"))
    } else {
        Ok(a / b)
    }
}
```

2. Write Unit Tests

Now, let's write unit tests for the calculator functions. In `src/lib.rs`, add the following test module:

```rust
rust

#[cfg(test)]
mod tests {
    use super::*;

    #[test]
    fn test_add() {
        assert_eq!(add(2, 3), 5);
    }

    #[test]
    fn test_subtract() {
        assert_eq!(subtract(5, 3), 2);
    }

    #[test]
    fn test_multiply() {
        assert_eq!(multiply(2, 3), 6);
    }

    #[test]
    fn test_divide() {
        assert_eq!(divide(6, 3), Ok(2));
        assert_eq!(divide(2, 0), Err("Division by
zero".to_string()));
    }
}
```

3. Benchmark the Calculator Operations

Next, let's benchmark the performance of the calculator operations using Criterion. Create a file `benches/benchmark.rs`:

```rust
rust

use criterion::{black_box, criterion_group,
criterion_main, Criterion};
use my_project::add;

fn bench_addition(c: &mut Criterion) {
    c.bench_function("addition", |b| {
```

```
            b.iter(|| add(black_box(2), black_box(3)))
    });
}

criterion_group!(benches, bench_addition);
criterion_main!(benches);
```

This benchmark tests the performance of the `add` function.

4. Run Tests and Benchmarks

Run the tests using:

bash

```
cargo test
```

Run the benchmarks using:

bash

```
cargo bench
```

Conclusion

In this chapter, we covered how to test and benchmark Rust code, which is essential for writing reliable and efficient software. We learned about Rust's built-in testing framework, which supports unit tests, integration tests, and property-based testing. We also explored **Criterion**, a powerful library for benchmarking, and applied it to measure the performance of the arithmetic operations in our **calculator** application.

Chapter 15: Rust in the Real World: From Small Projects to Production Systems

---

Overview: Transition from Learning Rust to Using It in Large-Scale Systems

As you've worked through the fundamentals of **Rust**, you've gained a solid foundation in its syntax, core features, and best practices. Now, it's time to transition from smaller, isolated projects to building **real-world systems**. Whether you're writing performance-critical software, building high-availability applications, or integrating Rust with other languages, this chapter will guide you through the process of applying Rust in large-scale systems.

Rust's unique combination of **performance, safety**, and **concurrency** makes it an excellent choice for writing scalable and efficient applications. From **system-level programming** to **web services** and **cloud deployments**, Rust provides the tools to handle complex, high-performance tasks while ensuring memory safety without the need for garbage collection.

In this chapter, we will cover how to design and build production-level systems with Rust, how to integrate it with other languages like C, and how to deploy Rust applications to the cloud. You'll also get hands-on experience by building a **real-world microservice** using Rust and integrating it with a front-end application.

By the end of this chapter, you will have the knowledge to take your Rust skills and build systems that can scale, integrate with other components, and run in production environments.

Designing Systems with Rust: Performance and Safety

Rust is known for its strong **performance** and **safety** guarantees. These qualities make it ideal for writing software that is both fast and reliable. In large-scale systems, these qualities are crucial because they allow you to build applications that can handle high loads, complex operations, and critical tasks, all while avoiding common issues like memory leaks and data races.

1. Performance Considerations in Rust

Rust's performance is on par with low-level languages like **C** and **C++**. Unlike garbage-collected languages, Rust uses its **ownership** and **borrowing** system to ensure memory is managed efficiently without runtime overhead. This makes Rust a great choice for performance-critical systems where low latency and high throughput are required.

Some performance features of Rust include:

- **Zero-cost abstractions**: Rust's abstractions, such as iterators, closures, and async/await, are designed in such a way that they introduce no additional runtime overhead compared to hand-written, low-level code.
- **Direct control over memory**: Rust provides fine-grained control over memory allocation and deallocation, which is crucial for systems programming.

- **Optimized for concurrency**: Rust's ownership and concurrency models make it safe to write concurrent code without introducing data races or undefined behavior.

When designing systems with Rust, consider the following aspects to ensure performance:

- **Concurrency**: Rust's **ownership system** ensures that your concurrent code is free from data races, making it easier to write safe, high-performance multi-threaded applications.
- **Memory management**: Rust's **no garbage collection** model gives you fine-grained control over how memory is allocated and deallocated.
- **Low-level control**: Rust allows you to directly manage resources, such as memory buffers, and work with hardware-level operations when necessary.

2. Safety Considerations in Rust

Safety is a key focus of Rust's design, especially when building large-scale systems. **Rust's ownership model** prevents common programming errors like null pointer dereferencing, memory leaks, and data races. This is especially important in **systems programming**, where bugs can lead to catastrophic failures or security vulnerabilities.

Rust's safety features include:

- **Ownership**: Each piece of data in Rust has a single owner, and ownership is transferred explicitly. This ensures that data is never accessed after being freed or used in multiple places concurrently.

- **Borrowing**: Rust enforces **immutable** or **mutable** borrowing rules, ensuring that data is either shared read-only or uniquely owned, but never both at the same time.
- **No undefined behavior**: Rust's strict type system and memory safety features ensure that you can't accidentally create unsafe conditions like buffer overflows or out-of-bounds access.

When building systems with Rust, safety is built into the language by default. The compiler helps you catch errors during development rather than at runtime, leading to more reliable and maintainable systems.

Integration with C and Other Languages

Rust's powerful **FFI (Foreign Function Interface)** capabilities allow it to integrate seamlessly with **C** and other languages, making it a great choice for projects that require interacting with existing libraries or legacy code. Many large-scale systems, especially those written in C or C++, require modern languages like Rust to improve safety and performance.

1. Calling C Functions from Rust

One of the most common integrations for Rust is with **C**, as many embedded systems, operating systems, and other high-performance applications are written in C. Rust provides tools to call C functions using `extern` blocks and the `bindgen` tool to generate bindings.

Here's an example of how you might call a C function from Rust:

```c
// C code (example.c)
#include <stdio.h>

void hello_from_c() {
    printf("Hello from C!\n");
}
```

Now, create the Rust bindings:

```rust
// Rust code (lib.rs)
extern "C" {
    fn hello_from_c();
}

fn main() {
    unsafe {
        hello_from_c();
    }
}
```

Explanation:

- The `extern "C"` block tells Rust that this function is written in C, and it specifies the function signature.
- The `unsafe` block is required because calling C functions involves dealing with raw pointers and potentially unsafe operations.

You can compile and link the C code with the Rust code using `cargo build`. This enables Rust to call C functions and libraries as part of the system, allowing you to take advantage of existing C libraries or system-level functionality.

2. Using Rust to Build Safe APIs for C Code

Rust is often used to build **safe APIs** that wrap unsafe C code, providing the performance benefits of C while ensuring memory safety. A typical pattern is to write the performance-critical or low-level parts of an application in C, and then use Rust to create a high-level, safe API for interacting with that code.

For example, imagine a scenario where you have a legacy C library for image processing. You could wrap the C library in a Rust module to ensure safety while maintaining high performance. The result would be a Rust crate that can be used safely from other Rust code or even other languages, with the C code hidden behind a safe Rust API.

3. Binding to Other Languages

Rust can also interface with other languages such as **Python**, **JavaScript**, and **Go**. Using tools like **PyO3**, **Neon**, or **Rust's WebAssembly support**, you can write high-performance Rust modules that integrate with applications in these languages.

Deploying Rust Applications to the Cloud

Deploying Rust applications to the cloud is no different from deploying applications written in other languages, but the performance and safety guarantees of Rust make it an excellent choice for building highly available and reliable cloud services.

1. Containerization with Docker

One common approach to deploying Rust applications is
containerization. Docker is widely used for packaging
applications and running them in isolated environments.
Rust's small binary size makes it well-suited for running inside
containers.

Here's a simple Dockerfile for a Rust application:

```dockerfile
# Use the official Rust image
FROM rust:1.56 as builder

# Set the working directory
WORKDIR /usr/src/myapp

#  the source code
 . .

# Build the Rust project
RUN cargo install --path .

# Final image to run the application
FROM debian:bullseye-slim

# Install necessary runtime dependencies
RUN apt-get update && apt-get install -y libssl-dev

#  the compiled binary from the builder image
 --from=builder /usr/local/cargo/bin/myapp
/usr/local/bin/myapp

# Run the application
CMD ["myapp"]
```

Explanation:

- This Dockerfile uses multi-stage builds: the first stage (`builder`) compiles the Rust application, and the second stage creates a minimal image for running the binary.
- The final image only includes the compiled binary and any necessary runtime dependencies, reducing the size of the container.

2. Deploying to Cloud Platforms

Once your application is containerized, you can deploy it to any cloud platform that supports containers. Popular platforms like **AWS**, **Google Cloud**, and **Azure** offer services for running containerized applications.

For example, on **AWS**, you can deploy a Dockerized Rust application using **Elastic Beanstalk** or **ECS (Elastic Container Service)**. On **Google Cloud**, you can use **Google Kubernetes Engine (GKE)** to manage and scale your containers.

To deploy your container to **AWS ECS**, you would typically:

1. Push the container to **Amazon Elastic Container Registry (ECR)**.
2. Create a task definition for ECS, specifying the container image and resources.
3. Deploy the task to an ECS cluster for scalable, managed deployment.

3. Serverless Rust on the Cloud

Another way to deploy Rust applications to the cloud is using **serverless** architecture. Serverless frameworks like **AWS Lambda** and **Google Cloud Functions** support Rust, allowing you to deploy functions that automatically scale based on demand.

Rust can be compiled into small, fast executables that are perfect for serverless applications. With **AWS Lambda**, you can create a Rust function that handles HTTP requests, performs computation, or interacts with other AWS services.

Here's a simple AWS Lambda function in Rust:

```rust
use lambda_runtime::{handler_fn, Context, Error};
use serde_json::{Value, json};

async fn function_handler(event: Value, _: Context) -> Result<Value, Error> {
    Ok(json!({"message": "Hello from Lambda!", "event": event}))
}

#[tokio::main]
async fn main() -> Result<(), Error> {
    let func = handler_fn(function_handler);
    lambda_runtime::run(func).await?;
    Ok(())
}
```

Explanation:

- This code defines a basic AWS Lambda function that returns a greeting message and the event it received.
- The function is asynchronous and uses the `lambda_runtime` crate, which helps run Rust functions on AWS Lambda.

Hands-on Project: Build a Real-World Microservice Using Rust, Deploy It, and Integrate It with a Front-End Application

In this project, we will build a simple **microservice** using Rust, deploy it to the cloud, and integrate it with a front-end application.

1. Design the Microservice

Let's design a simple **task management** microservice. The microservice will allow users to create, read, update, and delete tasks.

We'll build the microservice with **Rocket**, a web framework for Rust, and connect it to a **PostgreSQL** database to store task data.

2. Set Up the Project

Start by creating a new Rust project:

bash

```
cargo new task_manager
cd task_manager
```

Add dependencies for Rocket and PostgreSQL:

toml

```
[dependencies]
rocket = "0.5"
rocket_contrib = "0.5"
serde = { version = "1.0", features = ["derive"] }
serde_json = "1.0"
diesel = { version = "1.4", features = ["postgres"] }
tokio = { version = "1", features = ["full"] }
```

3. Implement the Task Management API

In `src/main.rs`, write the API to handle tasks:

rust

```
#[macro_use] extern crate rocket;
use rocket_contrib::json::Json;
use serde::{Serialize, Deserialize};

#[derive(Serialize, Deserialize)]
struct Task {
    id: i32,
    description: String,
    completed: bool,
}

#[post("/tasks", format = "json", data = "<task>")]
fn create_task(task: Json<Task>) -> Json<Task> {
    // Save the task in the database (mocked)
    Json(task.into_inner())
}

#[launch]
fn rocket() -> _ {
    rocket::build().mount("/", routes![create_task])
}
```

4. Test the API Locally

Run the server with:

bash

```
cargo run
```

You can now send requests to the API using `curl` or Postman.

5. Deploy to the Cloud

Once the application is ready, you can **dockerize** the application and deploy it to a cloud provider like **AWS** or **Google Cloud**.

Conclusion

In this chapter, we explored how Rust can be used to design and build **real-world systems**, including microservices, using its performance and safety features. We also looked at how to integrate Rust with **C**, deploy applications to the cloud, and write efficient, safe code for production systems.

By applying the lessons from this chapter, you'll be well-equipped to take on larger, more complex projects in Rust, build **high-performance** systems, and deploy them to the cloud with confidence.

Conclusion: Your Path to Mastery in Rust

Review of Key Concepts Learned

As you come to the end of this book, it's essential to pause and reflect on the journey you've taken with Rust, the **systems programming language** known for its powerful combination of **performance**, **safety**, and **concurrency**. You've made substantial progress in learning how to use Rust to write fast, reliable, and concurrent software. Let's take a moment to review the key concepts you've mastered and how they fit together to create a strong foundation for building software in Rust.

1. The Core of Rust: Ownership and Borrowing

At the heart of Rust is its **ownership system**, which distinguishes it from other programming languages. Through the concepts of **ownership**, **borrowing**, and **lifetimes**, you've learned how Rust ensures memory safety without needing a garbage collector. This system prevents common errors such as memory leaks and data races, making your programs more reliable and efficient.

- **Ownership**: Every piece of data has a single owner. Once ownership is transferred, no other part of the program can access the data, preventing use-after-free errors.
- **Borrowing**: Rust allows data to be borrowed either **mutably** or **immutably**, but it ensures that these

borrows don't conflict with one another, avoiding race conditions.
- **Lifetimes**: Lifetimes ensure that references to data remain valid, preventing dangling pointers.

Mastering the ownership system is essential because it provides the **foundation** for safe and performant code, especially in complex and resource-constrained environments like embedded systems or high-concurrency applications.

2. Rust's Performance and Memory Management

Rust's performance is one of its most significant advantages. By enabling developers to have **fine-grained control over memory allocation** and deallocation, Rust allows you to write code that rivals low-level languages like C and C++, without sacrificing safety.

You've learned how Rust ensures performance with its zero-cost abstractions. These abstractions (e.g., iterators, closures, and async/await) allow you to write high-level code without introducing the runtime overhead typically associated with higher-level languages. The absence of a garbage collector means you can write **highly efficient systems** without worrying about performance degradation over time.

Rust's focus on **concurrency** also contributes to its performance. The ownership and borrowing model ensures that multiple threads can safely access memory without race conditions, which is essential in modern multi-core systems.

3. Concurrency and Asynchronous Programming in Rust

Rust's **concurrency** model is one of the language's standout features. You've learned that Rust makes writing **concurrent code** much safer and easier through its ownership model. **Concurrency** allows you to run multiple tasks in parallel, and Rust's safe concurrency guarantees mean that you won't face the issues like **data races** and **deadlocks** that often plague concurrent systems.

The introduction of **asynchronous programming** with **async/await** further extends Rust's concurrency model, enabling you to write **non-blocking** code. By understanding **async/await** and **futures**, you can now build applications that can handle thousands of I/O-bound tasks efficiently—whether it's a web server, an API service, or a database query handler.

4. Working with Traits and Generics

In Rust, **traits** and **generics** allow you to write flexible, reusable, and **type-safe** code. By mastering these features, you've learned to write functions and data structures that can work with any type, without compromising type safety.

- **Traits** allow you to define shared behavior across different types, enabling polymorphism. You can create generic code that works with any type that implements a particular trait, leading to highly reusable code.
- **Generics** allow you to define functions, structs, and enums that can work with multiple types, ensuring type safety while also making your code more flexible and reusable.

The combination of traits and generics enables you to write **clean**, **flexible**, and **type-safe** abstractions that can be used across different domains, from libraries to applications.

5. Macros and Metaprogramming

In Rust, **macros** provide a way to reduce repetitive code and write code that generates other code at compile time. You've seen how macros can be used to implement custom logic, reduce boilerplate, and even create complex functionalities that are difficult to implement using functions alone.

With macros, you've learned how to:

- Reduce repetitive code.
- Create custom DSLs (Domain-Specific Languages).
- Extend the language with **meta-programming** features.

While macros are a powerful tool, understanding when and how to use them is crucial. They allow for **flexible, reusable** code while still benefiting from Rust's strong **type-checking** and **safety guarantees**.

6. Error Handling in Rust

Rust's approach to error handling is robust and ensures that errors are handled explicitly, rather than silently ignored or left unhandled. You've learned about the **Result** and **Option** types, which are used to represent errors and optional values, respectively.

- The **Result** type is used for functions that can either succeed or fail, forcing you to handle possible errors at compile time.

- The **Option** type is used for values that may or may not exist, making it clear when values could be missing or absent.

Rust's error handling model emphasizes **explicitness** and **safety**, ensuring that errors are handled at the appropriate time and preventing **panic-driven** error propagation.

Next Steps After Finishing the Book: Continuous Learning and Community Involvement

Congratulations on completing this book! You've built a solid foundation in Rust, and you're now equipped to tackle more complex, real-world projects. However, the journey doesn't end here. Rust is a **dynamic language** with a vibrant and **active community**. To continue progressing in your Rust journey, here are some next steps:

1. Contribute to Open Source Projects

Rust has a **thriving open-source ecosystem**. Contributing to open source projects is one of the best ways to continue learning and building your skills. You can contribute by:

- Fixing bugs in Rust libraries.
- Writing documentation for Rust projects.
- Contributing new features or optimizing existing ones.

By contributing, you will get real-world experience with **large codebases, collaborative development**, and **best practices** for Rust programming. Many open-source Rust projects are always looking for contributors, and they provide a great opportunity to grow as a developer.

2. Participate in the Rust Community

The Rust community is one of the most welcoming and **helpful** programming communities. Joining the community will allow you to stay updated with the latest developments and ask for help when needed. You can participate in various ways:

- **Rust Forums**: Join the Rust user forum where you can ask questions, share experiences, and engage in discussions.
- **Rust Users Group**: Join a local or virtual Rust Users Group (RUG) in your area to meet other Rustaceans and collaborate on projects.
- **Rust Subreddits**: Follow the Rust subreddit to stay informed about new tutorials, blog posts, and community events.
- **Rust Discord/IRC**: Chat with fellow Rust developers in real-time, ask questions, or help others with their issues.

3. Keep Learning and Experimenting

Rust is a **highly versatile** language, and there are always new areas to explore. As you build more projects and dive deeper into Rust, here are a few areas where you can continue to grow:

- **WebAssembly**: Learn how to compile Rust code to WebAssembly for building **high-performance web applications**.
- **Embedded Systems**: Explore how Rust is being used in **embedded systems programming** and start working on low-level hardware projects.

- **Concurrency & Parallelism**: Further deepen your understanding of **async programming**, **concurrent systems**, and **parallel processing** in Rust.
- **Web Development**: Expand your knowledge of **web frameworks** like Rocket, Actix, or Tide to build robust, scalable web services and APIs.
- **Game Development**: Rust is gaining traction in game development, especially for **performance-intensive** games. Explore game engines like **Amethyst** and **Bevy**.

Encouragement to Keep Building and Innovating

At this point in your Rust journey, you have a wealth of tools, techniques, and knowledge at your disposal. **Rust** is a language that empowers you to build reliable, high-performance, and efficient systems, and the best way to truly master it is by **building real-world projects**.

Here are some ideas for projects that will help reinforce what you've learned and continue your development as a Rust programmer:

- **Build a Microservice**: Design and implement a microservice that communicates over HTTP and interacts with a database. This project will allow you to apply your knowledge of networking, databases, and asynchronous programming.
- **Write a Command-Line Tool**: Write a command-line utility that interacts with the file system, parses data, and performs complex operations. This will give you experience with working with external libraries and tools like `serde` and `clap`.

- **Develop an Embedded Application**: Start an embedded systems project using Rust, such as controlling an LED, managing sensors, or building a home automation system. This is a great way to get hands-on experience with low-level systems.
- **Create a Rust Web App**: Build a full-stack web application using Rust's web frameworks like Rocket or Actix. This project will give you experience in server-side programming, API design, and database integration.

The possibilities with Rust are **limitless,** and as you continue to build and innovate, you will deepen your understanding of its power. Rust is a language designed for those who want to write **fast**, **safe**, and **concurrent** systems, and you now have the knowledge to take on **complex projects** and **real-world challenges**.

Resources for Further Study: Books, Blogs, and Online Communities

As you continue your Rust journey, there are plenty of resources available to deepen your understanding and help you stay up to date with the latest Rust developments. Here's a curated list of **books, blogs**, and **communities** where you can continue learning:

1. Books

- **"The Rust Programming Language"**: Also known as **The Rust Book,** this is the official guide to Rust and an excellent starting point for new Rust developers. It's available for free online at https://doc.rust-lang.org/book/.

- **"Rust in Action"** by Tim McNamara: This book provides a hands-on, project-based approach to learning Rust, focusing on real-world examples and performance-critical applications.
- **"Programming Rust"** by Jim Blandy and Jason Orendorff: This is a comprehensive guide to Rust's systems programming capabilities. It dives deep into memory management, concurrency, and advanced features of the language.
- **"Rust by Example"**: This book provides examples of Rust syntax and functionality with detailed explanations and practical exercises. It's available online at https://doc.rust-lang.org/stable/rust-by-example/.

2. Blogs

- **The Rust Blog**: Stay updated with the latest news, features, and tutorials from the Rust team at https://blog.rust-lang.org/.
- **Rust by Example**: The official Rust documentation also includes a section called "Rust by Example," which presents Rust features through examples that you can experiment with in the Rust playground.
- **Rust Programming Blog**: Another great resource for Rust tutorials, tips, and updates. Check it out at https://rust-lang-nursery.github.io/rust-cookbook/.

3. Online Communities

- **The Rust Users Forum**: A place to discuss Rust, ask questions, and learn from others. Available at https://users.rust-lang.org/.

- **Rust Subreddit**: A thriving community of Rust enthusiasts who share news, resources, and questions. Visit https://www.reddit.com/r/rust/.
- **Rust Discord**: Join the Rust Discord server for real-time discussions and help with your Rust projects. Visit https://discord.com/invite/rust-lang.

Final Thoughts

Congratulations on completing this book and gaining a deep understanding of Rust! Whether you're building embedded systems, web applications, or performance-critical software, Rust provides a powerful and safe environment for creating robust applications.

By continuing to learn, building projects, and engaging with the Rust community, you'll keep growing your skills and stay at the cutting edge of systems programming. Remember, the journey of mastering Rust is ongoing, and the more you experiment, innovate, and collaborate, the more you'll uncover the true power of Rust.

Rust is a language built for the future of programming—fast, reliable, and safe. So, take the next step and continue your journey to **mastery**. Happy coding!

www.ingramcontent.com/pod-product-compliance
Lightning Source LLC
La Vergne TN
LVHW022343060326
832902LV00022B/4222